*A Book of Australian*
*Verse*

# A Book of
# Australian Verse

SELECTED AND WITH AN
INTRODUCTION BY

JUDITH WRIGHT

MELBOURNE
OXFORD UNIVERSITY PRESS
LONDON   WELLINGTON   NEW YORK
1968

*Oxford University Press, Ely House, London, W.1*

GLASGOW NEW YORK TORONTO MELBOURNE WELLINGTON
CAPE TOWN SALISBURY IBADAN NAIROBI LUSAKA ADDIS ABABA
BOMBAY CALCUTTA MADRAS KARACHI LAHORE DACCA
KUALA LUMPUR HONG KONG TOKYO

*Oxford University Press, 7 Bowen Crescent, Melbourne*

*National Library of Australia*
REGISTRY NUMBER AUS 67-542

*First published 1956*
*Reprinted 1962*
*Second edition 1968*

*Registered in Australia for transmission by post as a book*
PRINTED IN AUSTRALIA BY HALSTEAD PRESS, SYDNEY

# Contents

# CONTENTS

# CONTENTS

# CONTENTS

# Introduction

This anthology, which first appeared in 1956, has now been revised to take some account of verse written since then, and of changes in the scene of Australian poetry. No such collection, of course, can hope to do more than sketch the outline of a development most of whose features are quite outside its scope. Also, it is necessarily heavily weighted towards the most recent writers represented, since the level of poetic competence —if not necessarily of poetic importance—and the number of actual writers, has risen in proportion to the increase in Australia's own population and literacy.

It is important to remember that the first poet represented in the collection, Charles Harpur, was born in 1813 and the youngest, Geoffrey Lehmann, in 1940. Over that comparatively brief gap in time almost unbelievable changes have come about in all countries, but in this, perhaps, most of all. It has never been possible for Australian poets to draw on any common accepted background of tradition or literature, except that of England, and the literature of England has in many ways been a poor guide to interpreting a country and a kind of life quite alien from anything known to it. We still bring up our children on Shakespeare, Chaucer, Pope and Keats; Australian writing reaches them in a grudging trickle, if at all. All this has added immeasurably to the problems of Australian writers, and perhaps especially of Australian poets.

These difficulties have been many, and are still formidable enough. The most important, at least until recently, was the lack of any living link with the country itself. Australia was settled, in the first instance, by convicts, transported against their will, and soldiery and officials who never intended to make the place their home. Later came enterprising and

I

materially-minded men anxious to make money and return to England as soon as possible. Those of them who stayed here generally did so because the country had defeated them. A few came, certainly, out of hope for a new life, but their voices, like that of Charles Harpur, were generally overwhelmed by those of the self-seekers.

For many years, a conception of Australia as a country to be loved or valued for its own sake was rare and difficult to uphold among such men and their descendants. What did arise among them was, not a love of the country as such, but rather of the freedom its great distances provided—a freedom from all that was implied by the convict system and by the colony's dependent status. Australia became a reality to its white settlers, in the first place, through the chance of political independence which it offered them, rather than through any deep feeling for the land itself. Even today, exploitation is the keynote of its economy, and respect for the soil and its natural growth of plants and animals is generally subordinate to the chance of money-making, at whatever cost to the landscape and its future.

This forms no favourable climate for poetry, which needs a background in which emotional, as well as material, values are given their due weight; and the effect of this shallowness of roots is easily traceable in Australian writing, with its uneasy attempts to solve or to ignore the problem of our attitude to the country. We are only now developing a true local idiom and feeling, and its growth is so slow that many perceptive observers can see none at all. This, perhaps more than any other factor, has turned Australian writers from the direction of interpretive, sensitive and experimental writing towards a more obvious and vigorous descriptiveness, influenced to some extent by the 'bush balladists' of the nineteenth century, and still operative, with a difference, in the youngest writers represented here, such as Dawe and Murray.

The earliest writers to deserve the name of poet—Harpur, Kendall and a few others—left a surprising amount of work; much of it valuable in the attempt to develop a method of transmuting their surroundings into the forms of English verse, but little of any permanent poetic value. What they provided, and, indeed, what Harpur at least set out to provide, was a basis from which later poets might venture further into the unknown.

This basis was not, in any sense of the term, innovatory in technique or even in feeling. The problem, as they felt it to exist, was not that of adapting English verse-forms to the wholly new and strange country in which they found themselves, but rather that of forcing its essence into such forms. There was a great deal that would not go in at all; and the clash of the two elements, the harsh frontier-life and the cultivated literary form in which it was expressed, makes much of this early work into a literary curiosity.

Harpur, the first writer of importance, had one inestimable advantage over his nineteenth-century successors, in that he began to write early enough to be still under the influence of the early Romantics, in particular of Wordsworth. It is clear that the Wordsworthian attitude to nature would have been a tool of inestimable value in coming to terms early with the Australian scene, had it been used consistently and with intelligence. Harpur used it so in a few poems.

But his immediate disciple and follower, Kendall, a generation younger, fell upon evil days. The later nineteenth-century debasement of the romantic attitude had set in; in England, Wordsworth had given place to, at best, Tennyson, at worst, Tupper. Kendall had not the strength of vision nor the self-confidence which might have counteracted these weakening

3

influences; and the fact that he was hailed as Australia's first important poet, and had to try to respond to the pressures this entailed, did not help him. He finally found his way beyond this, but too late to produce work of much interest or importance.

During the nineteenth century, almost unnoticed, the nomadic bush workers and settlers were producing, as the early convicts had done, a currency of ballads and bush songs that was to issue into Australian literature with quite explosive effect. The first to see the possibilities of these ballads was Adam Lindsay Gordon; tamed, adapted and made to look decently artificial, he introduced them to polite society in 'The Sick Stockrider' and one or two other pieces of verse, and started a flood of ballads in city and country alike. Gordon himself, sentimental and swaggering, does not merit much consideration as a serious artist, but largely through the influence of this one poem, he achieved a greater immediate popularity than any Australian writer had enjoyed. The 'bush balladists' were soon swamped by the more literary '*Bulletin* bards', of whom Paterson, Lawson and Brady are the best remembered. Out of this development (and reinforced by Australian participation in the Boer War) emerged the Australian's idea of his own typical qualities of character— a kind of devil-may-care ironical swagger, self-conscious and adolescent enough, yet with elements of true masculinity. This attitude may be seen to colour the work of such writers as Slessor, Stewart, Campbell, Manifold, and FitzGerald, and even that of younger men like Dawe. Manifold's poem, 'The Tomb of Lt John Learmonth, A.I.F.', is a conveniently obvious illustration of their influence.

The problems of Australian poetry, on the other hand, were accentuated, after Kendall's failure to complete Harpur's work by helping to assimilate Australian life to the culture

Australians brought with them. The *fin de siècle* self-questioning of Europe and England had begun. Obvious cracks were beginning to appear in the tradition within which Harpur and Kendall had considered themselves as working. In addition, Australian national feeling was stirring, in the movement which culminated in Federation in the early years of the twentieth century; a new kind of radicalism, too, was finding expression in the work of Lawson and O'Dowd. The problem here resolved itself into two—the specifically poetic question of the right relationship of Australian to English and European poetry, and the local problem of the expression of Australian national and environmental values.

The first was exemplified by the appearance of Australia's first poet of more than regional importance—Christopher Brennan.

Brennan, a scholar and an admirer of contemporary French poetry, in particular that of Mallarmé, brought to his writing a sophistication of thought and a depth of culture which Australian verse had never yet approached, and has seldom equalled since. The conflict which is the central source of his poetry is that of the individual in relation to his world and further, to the universe: he sought to order his conception of life, so as to achieve the inner harmony for which he longed. Basically, then, his problem was that of the twentieth-century individual, whose values have dissolved in crisis. He is Australia's first truly 'modern' writer. It may be that the acuteness of the conflict in Brennan—so great as to end in personal tragedy—was accentuated by his lack of a critically informed audience and of a traditional background. His work has never been well known, and until recently it remained out of print and virtually unobtainable. The few lyrics given here cannot fitly represent his work, for his books were conceived as wholes and should be read as such.

5

Brennan's contemporary, Bernard O'Dowd, espoused the cause of nationalism, and attained a far greater reputation in his day; but unlike Brennan's his work has dated badly. His early themes were those of the rational-Socialist group, sprung of the theories of Darwin, Bradlaugh, and the Fabian group in England, which enjoyed great popularity among the young intellectuals of the first years of the century. His verse, particuarly that written earlier, was often mere doggerel, and even his best work is marred almost beyond reading by vicious habits of cliché and ranting, and by a fustian manner in which allegorical abstractions strut in capital letters. Though his long poem 'The Bush' has good passages, his work as a whole is that of a political patriot rather than of a scholar or poet in the true sense.

O'Dowd's popularity, contrasted with the long neglect of Brennan, gives a pointer to the general direction of Australian verse towards the objective rather than the subjective. Two notable figures of the first few decades of the twentieth century, however, stand aside from this rule, though they are wholly unlike each other.

The first, John Shaw Neilson, was a 'born rhymer', a simple man whose art seems to owe nothing to study. A labourer for much of his life (he worked in quarries and as a road-maker until friends found him a less physically exacting job in Melbourne), with little formal education and apparently little curiosity as to other poets' work, he composed his verses 'in his head', as and when he could, and much of his work was certainly lost for lack of opportunity to write it down. It is the lovely delicacy and sweetness of his best work which disarms one, striking the ear as strangely as a child's comment on the world. He has not the depth of feeling nor the observing eye of John Clare, to whom he has inevitably been compared: his quality is rather that of an untouched purity, of a spring-like vision as natural as the flowering of his own white Plum Tree.

The second, William Baylebridge, was philosopher as much as—at times more than—poet, and his recluse life and dedication to his work make him unique among Australian writers. Baylebridge's verse has been called obscure, his philosophy dismissed as Nietzschean. Neither judgement is entirely true; for when his books are read as organic wholes, as he intended them, what seems difficult in the single poem becomes easy to interpret, and his philosophy owes more to Bergson than to Nietzsche, in its emphasis on the 'life-force' and its treatment of time. Yet there is much of Nietzsche in Baylebridge, and unfortunately it is at the point where Nietzsche fails both as philosopher and as personality that Baylebridge most resembles him. He regarded himself as the prophet of Australia's rise to a nationalism which should express the upsurge and onward movement of this 'life-force', and his admiration for the qualities of leadership brought him to advocate something perilously close to totalitarianism. His almost Germanic earnestness of purpose, his advocacy of such unpopular causes as eugenics, his admiration for power, and its consequence in his leaning towards totalitarianism, have been oddly out of place in the Australian climate of feeling; it is to be hoped that they will remain so. Yet his verse, inflated and tortuous as it is, can rise to the tones of passionate and forceful sincerity.

The work of Hugh McCrae, influenced by Norman Lindsay and other members of Lindsay's immediate circle, represents a temporary reaction against the task of interpreting Australia, which had again been overtly taken up by Frank Wilmot ('Furnley Maurice'). Rather, McCrae in poetry, as Lindsay in his paintings, returned to the old Greek and Roman pantheisms for subjects. But these nymphs, centaurs and goddesses (not always convincingly re-imagined) achieved no real relationship with their new surroundings, and remain shapes of cardboard. Behind them, however, McCrae's own happy bacchanalianism and his light dancing rhythms attain a life of their own, and as a poet, though even his best work tends to be fragmentary and evanescent, McCrae attained at times to a high level of technical assurance.

Out of this period emerged Kenneth Slessor and Robert D. FitzGerald who, influenced by the Lindsay-McCrae group in their youth, have in their turn exerted a strong influence on later currents of writing in Australia.

Slessor, whose 'Five Visions of Captain Cook' is the progenitor of a good deal of verse, narrative and other, based on the early voyagers of the Pacific, and whose terse, pictorial, image-laden style and great technical proficiency set a new standard of versecraft here, has written little since the publication of his selected volume *One Hundred Poems*. FitzGerald, however, has continued to write, and has indeed gained strength. The publication of his *Forty Years' Poems* in 1965 proved that his meditative, involved, sometimes awkward gift has reached its height in work published over his later years.

FitzGerald is not everyone's poet, but his consistency of vision and plain sincerity of mind have done much to increase the sense here that poetry could be a calling, rather than, as with McCrae, a semi-private hobby. Hence, when in the war years a number of young poets began to publish, most of them took their craft seriously as a matter for professional and personal dedication, and many have continued to do so over the last quarter-century.

Among these are poets who, like David Campbell and Douglas Stewart, take their chief strength from that contemplation of natural themes in which, during the 'forties, Australian poetry overcame its problem of adaptation to the

Australian landscape. Over against them stand the poets who have become known as 'the academics', led by James McAuley and A. D. Hope, both influential neo-classicist writers. There are also the poets who have survived the phase of Jindyworobak theory and integrated it into their work, such as Roland Robinson and William Hart-Smith, and several women writers, Rosemary Dobson, Nan McDonald, and Judith Wright, all of whom began to publish in the decade that begins with 1937.

After the 'forties, the great increase in technology and industry in Australia resulted in considerable changes in outlook. The emphasis swung from country to city, and the number of universities and of university-trained young men and women began to rise impressively. This has meant that writers like Campbell are in temporary eclipse, and that the influence of Hope and McAuley (both now university professors) has been pre-eminent over the last decade. McAuley has lately turned to book-length narrative verse in *Captain Quiros*, a poem which sets Quiros' dream of establishing the New Jerusalem in the South Land against the realities of history and expresses McAuley's own faith in the final victory of the spiritual over modern materialism. Hope published his *Collected Poems* in 1965, and proved thereby that, while he and McAuley are alike in rejecting all verbal and technical poetic experiment in favour of an almost eighteenth-century verse-form and enunciation, their paths are otherwise very different. Both are deeply concerned by the present problems of humanity, but while McAuley sees the solution as an enlightened return to religious disciplines, Hope, more sceptical and satiric, inclines to a faith in an emergent creative solution within man himself, mediated partly at least by art.

Another important poet whose work began appearing in the war years, Francis Webb, though he has not attained the

9

reputation of Hope or McAuley, has published a number of books of obscure but remarkable poetry. His path has led through terrifying areas of experience, emerging here and there into brief spaces of calm and illumination; beyond the rest of Australian poets, he has lived through modern psychic problems as well as perceived them.

A considerable number of poets now in their thirties and forties can be represented here only by a few poems. The most important of them probably are Vincent Buckley, Gwen Harwood, Bruce Dawe and Randolph Stow. Buckley, often regarded as one of the 'academics', has turned lately to political poems which are much fiercer and more epigrammatic than his early verse, and has thereby influenced many younger poets. Neither Dawe nor Stow (though the latter is a university graduate) can be placed in that classification; Dawe, like Hope and Buckley, however, writes a good deal of pointed polemic verse. Stow, also well-known as a novelist, takes up the theme of the Australian landscape as an inner reality and a stage in the progress of the human search, much as Patrick White used it in *Voss* and Sidney Nolan in numerous paintings.

Other young poets have turned away from philosophical examination or psychological questioning towards a more immediate and even social approach, which uses the immediate observation as its starting-point, and deliberately refrains from going far into generalization. This hard-edged and matter-of-fact poetry is seen at its best in the work of Dawe and Simpson, who can handle large themes with its help as well as the portraits and lesser social comment that occupy many of the younger poets. It can perhaps be seen as a further extension of the balladic influence, via recent 'protest song' movements; though some of its products seem almost wilfully limited and trivial, it can also issue in such memorable and violent images of man's condition as Murray's 'The Burning Truck' and Lehmann's 'The Pigs'.

It is surprising that poetry so far seems little concerned with what is now Australia's chief problem—our relationship, or lack of relationship, to the cultures of the countries which are our nearest neighbours. Ever since the Colombo Plan was instituted, students have been coming from India, Indonesia, Malaysia and other Asian countries for education at universities here, in quite impressive numbers, and considering how many young poets are graduates or members of university staffs, some useful exchange might by now have been evident. None has, so far, appeared; nor has any important poetry issued from our involvements in Asian wars, except for a poem or two from non-participants. Perhaps the chief influence on poetry here will soon be that of the Americans; events seem to be forcing us in this direction, rather than towards the Asian cultures.

JUDITH WRIGHT

NORTH TAMBORINE
1967

## CHARLES HARPUR

### *A Midsummer Noon in the Australian Forest*

Not a sound disturbs the air,
There is quiet everywhere;
Over plains and over woods
What a mighty stillness broods!

All the birds and insects keep
Where the coolest shadows sleep;
Even the busy ants are found
Resting in their pebbled mound;
Even the locust clingeth now
Silent to the barky bough:
Over hills and over plains
Quiet, vast and slumbrous, reigns.

Only there's a drowsy humming
From yon warm lagoon slow coming:
'Tis the dragon-hornet—see!
All bedaubed resplendently,
Yellow on a tawny ground—
Each rich spot nor square nor round,
Rudely heart-shaped, as it were
The blurred and hasty impress there
Of a vermeil-crusted seal
Dusted o'er with golden meal.
Only there's a droning where
Yon bright beetle shines in air,

13

Tracks it in its gleaming flight
With a slanting beam of light,
Rising in the sunshine higher,
Till its shards flame out like fire.

Every other thing is still,
Save the ever-wakeful rill,
Whose cool murmur only throws
Cooler comfort round repose;
Or some ripple in the sea
Of leafy boughs, where, lazily,
Tired summer, in her bower
Turning with the noontide hour,
Heaves a slumbrous breath ere she
Once more slumbers peacefully.

O 'tis easeful here to lie
Hidden from noon's scorching eye,
In this grassy cool recess
Musing thus of quietness.

# DANIEL HENRY DENIEHY

## *To His Wife*

O pure of soul, and fond and deep of heart
    For those who darkened be,
Lift up thy holy voice at morn and eve
    And pray for me—

For me, who for this thronging world's hot strife
   A prize hath brought to be
Among the known—but sweet too dearly earned;
   Ah, pray for me.

Not aye the scholar's path a track of peace,
   Nor from the dread sins free;
Hard by the Isles of Truth doth Circe prowl;
   Oh, pray for me.

The spirit's hell-gloom and its hurricane
   Round studious cells may be;
Thou patient Moon of Memory's dreary sky,
   Oh, pray for me.

When through thy well-known window, open beneath
   The uneasy, whispering tree,
Burn stars we children two have tried to count,
   Then pray for me.

At hour of rest, and when the moon makes pleased
   The melancholy sea,
And noon's surcease of happy household toil,
   Yes, pray for me.

Some solace for this wrung and rifted heart,
   That, wheresoe'er thou be,
Thou wilt, God's holiest gift, thou woman pure,
   Yet pray for me.

## HENRY KENDALL

### *Prefatory Sonnet*

I purposed once to take my pen and write,
  Not songs, like some, tormented and awry
  With passion, but a cunning harmony
Of words and music caught from glen and height,
And lucid colours born of woodland light
  And shining places where the sea-streams lie.
But this was when the heat of youth glowed white,
  And since I've put the faded purpose by.
I have no faultless fruits to offer you
  Who read this book; but certain syllables
  Herein are borrowed from unfooted dells
And secret hollows dear to noontide dew;
And these, at least, though far between and few,
  May catch the sense like subtle forest spells.

## WILLIAM GAY

### *The Crazy World*

The World did say to me,
  'My bread thou shalt not eat,
I have no place for thee
  In house nor field nor street.

'I have no land nor sea
  For thee, nor home nor bread;
I scarce can give to thee
  A grave when thou art dead.'

16

'O crazy World,' said I,
  'What is it thou canst give,
Which wanting, I must die,
  Or having, I shall live?

'When thou thy all hast spent,
  And all thy harvests cease,
I still have nutriment
  That groweth by decrease.

'Thy streets will pass away,
  Thy towers of steel be rust,
Thy heights to plains decay,
  Thyself be whirling dust;

'But I go ever on
I mount from prime to prime,
From an eternal throne
  I govern Chance and Time.

'Then, crazy World,' said I,
  'What is it thou canst give,
Which wanting, I must die,
  Or having, I shall live?'


BARCROFT HENRY BOAKE

*Where the Dead Men Lie*

Out on the wastes of the Never Never—
That's where the dead men lie!
There where the heat waves dance for ever—
That's where the dead men lie!

17

C

That's where the Earth's loved sons are keeping
Endless tryst: not the west wind sweeping
Feverish pinions can wake their sleeping—
Out where the dead men lie!

Where brown Summer and Death have mated—
That's where the dead men lie!
Loving with fiery lust unsated—
That's where the dead men lie!
Out where the grinning skulls bleach whitely
Under the saltbush sparkling brightly;
Out where the wild dogs chorus nightly—
That's where the dead men lie!

Deep in the yellow, flowing river—
That's where the dead men lie!
Under the banks where the shadows quiver—
That's where the dead men lie!
Where the platypus twists and doubles,
Leaving a train of tiny bubbles;
Rid at last of their earthly troubles—
That's where the dead men lie!

East and backward pale faces turning—
That's how the dead men lie!
Gaunt arms stretched with a voiceless yearning—
That's how the dead men lie!
Oft in the fragrant hush of nooning,
Hearing again their mothers' crooning,
Wrapt for aye in a dreamful swooning—
That's how the dead men lie!

Only the hand of Night can free them—
That's when the dead men fly!

Only the frightened cattle see them—
See the dead men go by!
Cloven hoofs beating out one measure,
Bidding the stockmen know no leisure—
That's when the dead men take their pleasure!
That's when the dead men fly!

Ask, too, the never-sleeping drover:
He sees the dead pass by;
Hearing them call to their friends—the plover,
Hearing the dead men cry;
Seeing their faces stealing, stealing,
Hearing their laughter pealing, pealing,
Watching their grey forms wheeling, wheeling
Round where the cattle lie!

Strangled by thirst and fierce privation—
That's how the dead men die!
Out on Moneygrub's farthest station—
That's how the dead men die!
Hard-faced greybeards, youngsters callow,
Some mounds cared for, some left fallow,
Some deep down, yet others shallow;
Some having but the sky.

Moneygrub, as he sips his claret,
Looks with complacent eye
Down at his watch-chain, eighteen-carat—
There, in his club, hard by
Recks not that every link is stamped with
Names of the men whose limbs are cramped with
Too long lying in grave-mould, camped with
Death where the dead men lie.

# BERNARD O'DOWD

## *Love and Sacrifice*

Can we not consecrate
 To man and God above
This volume of our great
 Supernal tide of love?

'Twere wrong its wealth to waste
 On merely me and you,
In selfish touch and taste
 As other lovers do.

This love is not as theirs:
 It came from the Divine,
Whose glory still it wears,
 And print of whose design.

The world is full of woe,
 The time is blurred with dust,
Illusions breed and grow,
 And eyes' and flesh's lust.

The mighty league with Wrong
 And stint the weakling's bread;
The very lords of song
 With Luxury have wed.

Fair Art deserts the mass,
 And loiters with the gay;
And only gods of brass
 Are popular today.

Two souls with love inspired,
　　Such lightning love as ours,
Could spread, if we desired,
　　Dismay among such powers.

Could social stables purge
　　Of filth where festers strife:
Through modern baseness surge
　　A holier tide of life.

Yea, two so steeped in love
　　From such a source, could draw
The angels from above
　　To lead all to their Law.

We have no right to seek
　　Repose in rosy bower,
When Hunger thins the cheek
　　Of childhood every hour:

Nor while the tiger, Sin,
　　'Mid youths and maidens roams,
Should Duty skulk within
　　These selfish cosy homes.

Our place is in the van
　　With those crusaders, who
Maintain the rights of man
　　'Gainst Despot and his crew.

If sacrifice may move
　　Their load of pain from men,
The greatest right of Love
　　Is to renounce It then.

Ah, Love, the earth is woe's,
  And sadly helpers needs:
And, till its burden goes,
  Our work is—where it bleeds.

# HENRY LAWSON

## *The Roaring Days*

The night too quickly passes
And we are growing old,
So let us fill our glasses
And toast the Days of Gold;
When finds of wondrous treasure
Set all the South ablaze,
And you and I were faithful mates
All through the roaring days!

Then stately ships came sailing
From every harbour's mouth,
And sought the Land of Promise
That beaconed in the South;
Then southward streamed their steamers
And swelled their canvas full
To speed the wildest dreamers
E'er borne in vessel's hull.

Their shining Eldorado
Beneath the southern skies
Was day and night for ever
Before their eager eyes.

The brooding bush, awakened,
Was stirred in wild unrest,
And all the year a human stream
Went pouring to the West.


The rough bush roads re-echoed
The bar-room's noisy din,
When troops of stalwart horsemen
Dismounted at the inn.
And oft the hearty greetings
And hearty clasp of hands
Would tell of sudden meetings
Of friends from other lands.


And when the cheery camp-fire
Explored the bush with gleams,
The camping-grounds were crowded
With caravans of teams;
Then home the jests were driven,
And good old songs were sung,
And choruses were given
The strength of heart and lung.


Oft when the camps were dreaming,
And fires began to pale,
Through rugged ranges gleaming
Swept on the Royal Mail.
Behind six foaming horses,
And lit by flashing lamps,
Old Cobb and Co., in royal state,
Went dashing past the camps.

Oh, who would paint a gold-field,
And paint the picture right,
As old Adventure saw it
In early morning's light?
The yellow mounds of mullock
With spots of red and white,
The scattered quartz that glistened
Like diamonds in light;

The azure line of ridges,
The bush of darkest green,
The little homes of calico
That dotted all the scene.
The flat straw hats, with ribands
That old engravings show—
The dress that still reminds us
Of sailors, long ago.

I hear the fall of timber
From distant flats and fells,
The pealing of the anvils
As clear as little bells,
The rattle of the cradle,
The clack of windlass-boles
The flutter of the crimson flags
Above the golden holes.

Ah, then their hearts were bolder,
And if Dame Fortune frowned
Their swags they'd lightly shoulder
And tramp to other ground.

Oh, they were lion-hearted
Who gave our country birth!
Stout sons, of stoutest fathers born,
From all the lands on earth!

Those golden days are vanished,
And altered is the scene;
The diggings are deserted,
The camping-grounds are green;
The flaunting flag of progress
Is in the West unfurled,
The mighty Bush with iron rails
Is tethered to the world.

## CHRISTOPHER BRENNAN

### *We Woke Together*

We woke together on a gusty dawn
in the dim house amid the level waste
and stared in anguish on the stretch of years
filled with grey dawn and ever-weeping wind.

For as the hour hung still 'twixt night and day
we whom the dark had drawn so close together
at that dead tide as strangers saw each other
strangers divided by a waste of years.

We might not weep out our passion of despair
but in lorn trance we gazed upon each other
and wondered what strange ways had brought our hands
together in that chamber of the west.

25

We felt the dumb compulsion of the hour
to wander forth in spirit on the wind
and drift far apart in undiscovered realms
of some blank world where dawn for ever wept.


## Let us Go Down

Let us go down, the long dead night is done,
the dolorous incantation has been wrought,
Soul, let us go, the saving word is won,
down from the tower of our hermetic thought.

See, for the wonder glimmers in the gates
eager to burst the soundless bars and grace
the wistful earth, that still in blindness waits
perfect with suffering for her Lord's embrace.

The spaces of the waters of the dawn
are spiritual with our transfigured gaze;
the intenser heights of morning, far withdrawn,
expect our dream to shine along their ways.

But speak the word! and o'er the adoring whole
straight from the marge of the perfected hours
sudden, large music through the vast, shall roll
a sea of light foaming with seedless flowers;

lilies that form on some ethereal wave
still generate of the most ancient blue,
burst roses rootless, knowing not the grave
nor yet the charnel thought by which they grew.

So we shall move at last, untortured powers,
and in white silence hear, as souls unborn,
our hymn given back by the eternal Hours
singing together in the eternal morn.


## Sweet Silence after Bells

Sweet silence after bells!
deep in the enamour'd ear
sweet incantation dwells.

Filling the rapt still sphere
a liquid crystal swims,
precarious yet clear.

Those metal quiring hymns
shaped ether so succinct:
a while, or it dislimns,

the silence, wanly prinkt
with forms of lingering notes,
inhabits, close, distinct;

and night, the angel, floats
on wings of blessing spread
o'er all the gathered cotes

where meditation, wed
with love, in gold-lit cells,
absorbs the heaven that shed

sweet silence after bells.

## My Heart was Wandering

My heart was wandering in the sands
a restless thing, a scorn apart;
Love set his fire in my hands,
I clasped the flame into my heart.

Surely, I said, my heart shall turn
one fierce delight of pointed flame,
and in that holocaust shall burn
its old unrest of scorn and shame.

Surely my heart the heavens at last
shall storm with fiery orisons
and know, enthroned in the vast,  *infinite, peaceful*
the fervid peace of molten suns.

The flame that feeds upon my heart
fades or flares, by wild winds controlled;
my heart still walks a thing apart,
my heart is restless as of old.  *held down by*
                                  *the finite*

## The Years that Go to Make Me Man

The years that go to make me man
this day are told a score and six
that should have set me magian
o'er my half-souls that struggle and mix.

But wisdom still remains a star
just hung within my aching ken,
and common prudence dwells afar
among contented homes of men.

28

In wide revolt and ruin tost
against whatever is or seems,
my futile heart still wanders lost
in the same vast and impotent dreams.

On either hand life hurries by
its common joy, its common mirth;
I reach vague hands of sympathy
a ghost upon this common earth.

## What Do I Know?

What do I know? myself alone,
a gulf of uncreated night,
wherein no star may e'er be shown
save I create it in my might.

What have I done? Oh foolish word,
and foolish deed your question craves!
Think ye the sleeping depths are stirred
though tempest hound the maddened waves?

What do I seek? I seek the word
that shall become the deed of might
whereby the sullen gulfs are stirred
and stars begotten on their night.

## *How Old is My Heart?*

How old is my heart, how old, how old is my heart?
and did I ever go forth with song when the morn was new?
I seem to have trod on many ways, I seem to have left
I know not how many homes; and to leave each
was still to leave a portion of mine own heart,
of my old heart whose life I had spent to make that home.
So I sit and muse in this wayside harbour and wait
till I hear the gathering cry of the ancient winds and again
I must up and out and leave the embers of the hearth
to crumble silently into white ash and dust,
and see the road stretch bare and pale before me: again
my garment and my home shall be the enveloping winds
and my heart be filled wholly with their old pitiless cry.

## *O Desolate Eves*

O desolate eves along the way, how oft,
despite your bitterness, was I warm at heart!
not with the glow of remembered hearths, but warm
with the solitary unquenchable fire that burns
a flameless heat deep in his heart who has come
where the formless winds plunge and exult for aye
among the naked spaces of the world,
far past the circle of the ruddy hearths
and all their memories. Desperate eves,
when the wind-bitten hills turned violet
along their rims, and the earth huddled her heat
within her niggard bosom, and the dead stones

lay battle-strewn before the iron wind
that, blowing from the chill west, made all its way
a loneliness to yield its triumph room;
yet in that wind a clamour of trumpets rang,
old trumpets, resolute, stark, undauntable,
singing to battle against the eternal foe,
the wronger of this world, and all his powers
in some last fight, foredoomed disastrous,
upon the final ridges of the world:
a war-torn note, stern fire in the stricken eve,
and fire thro' all my ancient heart, that sprang
towards that last hope of a glory won in defeat,
whence, knowing not sure if such high grace befall
at the end, yet I draw courage to front the way.


## I Said, This Misery Must End

I said, This misery must end:
Shall I, that am a man and know
that sky and wind are yet my friend,
sit huddled under any blow?
so speaking left the dismal room
and stepped into the mother-night
all filled with sacred quickening gloom
where the few stars burned low and bright,
and darkling on my darkling hill
heard thro' the beaches' sullen boom
heroic note of living will
ring trumpet-clear against the fight;
so stood and heard, and raised my eyes
erect, that they might drink of space,
and took the night upon my face,

31

till time and trouble fell away
and all my soul sprang up to feel
as one among the stars that reel
in rhyme on their rejoicing way,
breaking the elder dark, nor stay
but speed beyond each trammelling gyre
till time and sorrow fall away
and night be withered up, and fire
consume the sickness of desire.

## JOHN SHAW NEILSON

### Song be Delicate

Let your song be delicate.
    The skies declare
No war—the eyes of lovers
    Wake everywhere.

Let your voice be delicate.
    How faint a thing
Is Love, little Love crying
    Under the Spring.

Let your song be delicate.
    The flowers can hear:
Too well they know the tremble
    Of the hollow year.

Let your voice be delicate.
    The bees are home:
All their day's love is sunken
    Safe in the comb.

Let your song be delicate.
  Sing no loud hymn:
Death is abroad . . . oh, the black season!
  The deep—the dim!


## To a Blue Flower

I would be dismal with all the fine pearls of the crown of a
    king;
But I can talk plainly to you, you little blue flower of the
    Spring!

Here in the heart of September the world that I walk in is full
Of the hot happy sound of the shearing, the rude heavy scent
    of the wool.

Soon would I tire of all riches or honours or power that they
    fling;
But you are my own, of my own folk, you little blue flower of
    the Spring!

I was around by the cherries to-day; all the cherries are pale:
The world is a woman in velvet: the air is the colour of ale.

I would be dismal with all the fine pearls of the crown of a
    king;
But I can give love-talk to you, you little blue flower of the
    Spring!


33

## Break of Day

The stars are pale.
Old is the Night, his case is grievous,
   His strength doth fail.

Through stilly hours
The dews have draped with Love's old lavishness
   The drowsy flowers.

And Night shall die,
Already, lo! the Morn's first ecstasies
   Across the sky.

An evil time is done.
Again, as someone lost in a quaint parable,
   Comes up the Sun.

## 'Tis the White Plum Tree

It is the white Plum Tree
   Seven days fair
As a bride goes combing
   Her joy of hair.

As a peacock dowered
   With golden eyes
Ten paces over
   The Orange lies.

34

It is the white Plum Tree
   Her passion tells,
As a young maid rustling,
   She so excels.

The birds run outward,
   The birds are low,
Whispering in manna
   The sweethearts go.

It is the white Plum Tree
   Seven days fair
As a bride goes combing
   Her joy of hair.

## The Orange Tree

The young girl stood beside me. I
   Saw not what her young eyes could see:
—A light, she said, not of the sky
   Lives somewhere in the Orange Tree.

—Is it, I said, of east or west?
   The heartbeat of a luminous boy
Who with his faltering flute confessed
   Only the edges of his joy?

Was he, I said, borne to the blue
   In a mad escapade of Spring
Ere he could make a fond adieu
   To his love in the blossoming?

35

—Listen! the young girl said. There calls
　No voice, no music beats on me;
But it is almost sound: it falls
　This evening on the Orange Tree.

—Does he, I said, so fear the Spring
　Ere the white sap too far can climb?
See in the full gold evening
　All happenings of the olden time?

Is he so goaded by the green?
　Does the compulsion of the dew
Make him unknowable but keen
　Asking with beauty of the blue?

—Listen! the young girl said. For all
　Your hapless talk you fail to see
There is a light, a step, a call,
　This evening on the Orange Tree.

—Is it, I said, a waste of love
　Imperishably old in pain,
Moving as an affrighted dove
　Under the sunlight or the rain?

Is it a fluttering heart that gave
　Too willingly and was reviled?
Is it the stammering at a grave,
　The last word of a little child?

—Silence! the young girl said. Oh, why,
　Why will you talk to weary me?
Plague me no longer now, for I
　Am listening like the Orange Tree.

## Stony Town

If ever I go to Stony Town, I'll go as to a fair,
With bells and men and a dance-girl with the heat-wave in her
      hair:
I'll ask the birds that live on the road; for I dream (though it
      may not be)
That the eldest song was a forest thought and the singer was a
      tree.

Oh, Stony Town is a hard town! It buys and sells and buys:
It will not pity the plights of youth or any love in the eyes:
No curve they follow in Stony Town; but the straight line and
      the square:
—And the girl shall dance them a royal dance, like a blue wren
      at his prayer.

Oh, Stony Town is a hard town! It sells and buys and sells:
—Merry men three I will take with me, and seven and twenty
      bells:
The bells will laugh and the men will laugh, and the girl shall
      shine so fair
With the scent of love and cinnamon dust shaken out of her
      hair.

Her skirts shall be of the gossamer, full thirty inches high;
And her lips shall move as the flowers move to see the winds go
      by:
The men will laugh, and the bells will laugh, to find the world
      so young;
And the girl shall go as a velvet bird, with a quick-step on her
      tongue.

She shall cry aloud that a million moons for a lover is not long,
And her mouth shall be as the green honey in the honey-
   eater's song:
If ever I go to Stony Town, I'll go as to a fair,
And the girl shall shake with the cinnamon and the heat-wave
   in her hair.


## Schoolgirls Hastening

Fear it has faded and the night:
   The bells all peal the hour of nine:
The schoolgirls hastening through the light
   Touch the unknowable Divine.

What leavening in my heart would bide!
   Full dreams a thousand deep are there:
All luminants succumb beside
   The unbound melody of hair.

Joy the long timorous takes the flute:
   Valiant with colour songs are born:
Love the impatient absolute
   Lives as a Saviour in the morn.

Get thou behind me, Shadow-Death!
   Oh ye Eternities, delay!
Morning is with me, and the breath
   Of schoolgirls hastening down the way.

## *I Spoke to the Violet*

Shy one, I said, you can take me away in a breath,
But I like not the coat that you come in—the colour of death.

The silence you come with is sweeter to me than a sound,
But I love not the colour—I saw it go into the ground.

And, though you haunt me with all that is health to a rhyme,
My thoughts are as old as the naked beginning of Time.

Your scent does encompass all beauty in one loving breath,
But I like not the coat that you come in—the colour of death.

## WILL DYSON

## *Death is but Death*

There is no soft beatitude in Death:
   Death is but Death;
   Nor can I find
   Him pale and kind
Who set that endless silence on her breath.
   Death is but Death!

There is no hidden comeliness in grief:
   Grief is but Grief;
   Nor for thy ill
   Canst thou distil
An unguent from the laurel's bitter leaf.
   Grief is but Grief!

There is no potent anodyne in tears:
  Tears are but Tears;
  Nor can the woe
  Of green wounds grow
Less green for their salt kindness through the years.
  Tears are but Tears!

## LEON GELLERT

### Before Action

We always had to do our work at night.
I wondered why we had to be so sly.
I wondered why we couldn't have our fight
Under the open sky.

I wondered why I always felt so cold.
I wondered why the orders seemed so slow,
So slow to come, so whisperingly told,
So whisperingly low.

I wondered if my packing-straps were tight,
And wondered why I wondered. Sound went wild . . .
An order came . . . I ran into the night
Wondering why I smiled.

### In the Trench

Every night I sleep
  And every night I dream
That I'm strolling with my sheep
  By the old stream.

Every morn I wake,
   And every morn I stand
And watch the shrapnel break
   On the smashed land.

Some night I'll fall asleep
   And will not wake at dawn.
I'll lie and feed my sheep
   On a green Lawn.

## These Men

Men moving in a trench, in the clear noon,
   Whetting their steel within the crumbling earth;
Men, moving in a trench 'neath a new moon
   That smiles with a slit mouth and has no mirth;
Men moving in a trench in the grey morn,
   Lifting bodies on their clotted frames;
Men with narrow mouths thin-carved in scorn
   That twist and fumble strangely at dead names.

These men know life—know death a little more,
   These men see paths and ends, and see
Beyond some swinging open door
   Into eternity.

FURNLEY MAURICE (Frank Wilmot)

## *To God: From the Warring Nations* (Selections)

### II

We pray for pity, Lord, not justice, we
   Being but mortal, offer mortal tears,
For justice would mean further cruelty,
   And we have had enough inhuman years.
Guard our repute! We have grown gross and mean,
Who hoped to tell the future something clean!
We come debauched, hoping and hoping not,
   Drunken with blood, burdened with all distress,
Craving for pity, Lord, who have forgot
   The name and manner of sweet gentleness.
We being mortal, love may come again;
Hold back severity—we are but men.
Ah! pity, Lord! Can all indulgence find
   Hope in the devious, devil-ways to Peace,
Of shamefaced, shuddering remnants of mankind
   All murdering, none brave enough to cease?
Redeem us by Thy hope, lest Thy disgust
Makes future empires violate our dust.

### III

We've smashed the tablets and the songs, forsworn
   The passionate sweet pity that once reigned
Imperial; must constant fear suborn
   The hearts that guilt and grossness have so stained?
Could we be as we were ere battle came,
We would not talk of guile or separate blame.

Search not our records for the first dark ruse,
    Let the past go, sin is an old affair;
We plead for pity, Lord, not for our dues,
    We, being sinners all, must share and share.
Let us, all sinners, and all stained with blood,
    Weary with bitter consciences and lies,
Assemble in a sinners' brotherhood
    And pour out tears from our repentant eyes,
Tears for such wrongs that only tears repair.


V

We have been cruel in thought. Life's not so sweet
    With pearls and pleasures that the race should set
Its ardour to destruction. Brutal feet
    Destroy the roses. God, let us forget
That we accused of barbarous intent
The foe that lies in death magnificent.
How can we hate forever, having proved
All men are bright and brave and somewhere loved?
For every man has courage, all are peerless;
    Each man reigns in his region, sovereign, free;
But we have broken blessed men and fearless,
    Each in his deep and separate agony.
We have cast curses upon unknown names,
    And we have fallen from our vows and Thee,
Gazed tearlessly on tortured human frames,
    And manacled the tongue of equity.
Oh, we have murdered hope and babes and things
Wrought by inspired fingers joyously;
Earth and her vines may shroud our murderings,
    But what shall kill immortal memory?

## XV

Thou gavest steel to us, Thou gavest brain,
　　Thou gavest patience; we grew grossly great;
And we have used Thy steel Thy will to chain,
　　But Thou hast burst those bonds; now we await
Thy judgement, who have meddled with Thy things.
　　We thought to snare the sacred flame from Thee—
Look on our broken hands, our withered wings,
　　And pity, Lord, our poor humanity.

# *The Gully* (Selections)

## II

Looking from the hut door one dawn in June
I saw Australian snow under the moon;
Tall ghostly gums in glacial silence dressed
Towered in eternal rest;
A mass of silver fog, a floating shroud,
Rolled slowly up the hillside to the crest
Like Silence going home into its cloud.
A woodman humped his pack and sauntered west,
Uphill into the sky,
Where all things go that die
Like flame and sound, and mist and minstrelsy.

## VII

There breaks upon my sight
　　A low magnificent light
Green as the core that in a green fire burns;
　　Each leaf is a green lamp, glowing,
　　Swung to illume my going
Down the moist colonnades of mouldering ferns.

44

Here is a spirit deep,
  Stirring in lonely sleep,
The windswept hills have heard my nameless fear;
  Till by great love oppressed
  I stilled my heart's unrest,
And spoke my love, and speech has brought its tear.

There is a spirit bound
  Within this holy ground;
A chrysalis cares not what freedom brings,
  But, without love or sight,
  Breaks its way into light
Not knowing it will some day move with wings.

## X

If I could take your mountains in my heart
And tell the wonder in another land,
As to some mariner mumbling o'er a chart
Strangers would hearken and not understand.
For you, without a poet or a past,
Await establishment; the years seem long
While we by hope and search, by feast and fast,
Prepare the passage for our king of song.
He will not suddenly burst into our day,
He will not come till we have cut the way.
'Tis more than one man's life to strike the reef,
To delve the precious ore, crush out the gold,
Hammer the metal into delicate leaf,
Or link by precious link forge chains that hold
The wandering passions of men in one vast fold.

## The Victoria Markets Recollected
## in Tranquillity

### I

Winds are bleak, stars are bright,
Loads lumber along the night:
Looming, ghastly white,
A towering truck of cauliflowers sways
Out of the dark, roped over and packed tight
Like faces of a crowd of football jays.

The roads come in, roads dark and long,
To the knock of hubs and a sleepy song.
Heidelberg, Point Nepean, White Horse,
Flemington, Keilor, Dandenong,
Into the centre from the source.

Rocking in their seats
The worn-out drivers droop
When dawn stirs in the streets
And the moon's a silver hoop;
Come rumbling into the silent mart,
To put their treasure at its heart,
Waggons, lorries, a lame Ford bus,
Like ants along the arms of an octopus
Whose body is all one mouth; that pays them hard
And drives them back with less than a slave's reward.

*When Batman first at Heaven's command*
*Said, 'This is the place for a peanut-stand',*
*It must have been grand!*

46

## II

'Cheap today, lady; cheap today!'
Jostling water-melons roll
From fountains of Earth's mothering soul.
Tumbling from box and tray
Rosy, cascading apples play
Each with a glowing aureole
Caught from a split sun-ray.
'Cheap today, lady, cheap today.'
Hook the carcases from the dray!
(*Where the dun bees hunt in droves*
*Apples ripen in the groves.*)

An old horse broods in a Chinaman's cart
While from the throbbing mart
Go cheese and celery, pears and jam
In barrow, basket, bag, or pram
To the last dram the purse affords—
Food, food for the hordes!

Shuffling in the driven crush
The souls and the bodies cry,
Rich and poor, skimped and flush,
'Spend or perish, buy or die!'

Food, food for the hordes!
The Turksheads tumble on the boards.

There's honey at the dairy produce stall
Where the strung saveloys festooning fall;
Yielding and yellow, the beautiful butter blocks
Confront the poultryman's plucked Plymouth Rocks.

The butcher is gladly selling,
Chopping and slaughtering, madly yelling.
A bull-like bellow for captured sales,
A great crowd surges around his scales.
Slap down the joint.
The finger point
Wobbles and comes alive,
Springs round to twenty and back to five.
To him Creation's total aim
Is selling chops to a doubting dame.
And what will matter his steaks and joints,
The underdone and the overdone,
On the day when old Earth jumps the points
And swings into the sun?

Along the shadows, furtive, lone,
The unwashed terrier carries his week-end bone,
An old horse with a pointed hip
And dangling disillusioned under-lip
Stands in a harvest-home of cabbage-leaves
And grieves.
A lady by a petrol case,
With a far-off wounded look in her face
Says, in a voice of uncertain pitch,
'Muffins', or 'crumpets', I'm not sure which.
A pavement battler whines with half a sob,
'Ain't anybody got a bloody bob?'
Haunted by mortgages and overdrafts
The old horse droops between the shafts.
A smiling Chinaman upends a bag
And spills upon the bench with thunder-thud
(A nearby urchin trilling the newest rag)
Potatoes caked with loamy native mud.

Andean pinnacles of labelled jam.
The melting succulence of two-toothed lamb.
The little bands of hemp that truss
The succulent asparagus
That stands like tiny sheaves of purple wheat
Ready to eat.
Huge and alluring hams and rashered swine
In circular repetitive design.
Gobbling turkeys and ducks in crates,
Pups in baskets and trays of eggs;
A birdman turns and gloomily relates
His woes to a girl with impossible legs.

*When Batman first at Heaven's command*
*Stuck flag-staffs in this sacred strand . . .*
*We'll leave all that to the local band.*

### IV

Shuffling in the driven tide
The huddled people press,
Hoarding and gloating, having defied
Hunger, cold and nakedness
For a few days more—or less.
Is it nothing to you that pass?
Will you not pity their need?
Store beef fattens on stolen grass,
Brows grow dark with covetous greed,
Storm or manacle, cringe or pray,
There is no way but the money way.

Pouring suns, pouring heavens, pouring earth,
And the life-giving seas!
Treasure eternally flowing forth,
None greater than these!

49

E

Richness, colour and form,
Ripe flavours and juices rare!

Within men's hearts rises a deathless prayer
Deep as a spirit storm,
Giving thanks that the earth has offered such
(So grateful to the eye, so rich to touch)
Miraculous varieties of fare.

And yet that lamb with the gentle eye,
She had to die.
There have been foolish dreams
Of fishes pulled from reedy streams,
Of delicate earthly fruits
Being torn up by the roots—
But only the Mandragora screams.

Gentle curates and slaughtermen
Murder the cattle in the pen:
Body, Spirit, the Word, the Breath
Only survive by so much death.
The old horse with the pointed hip
And disillusioned under-lip
Stands in a drift of cabbage-leaves
And grieves.

# WILLIAM BAYLEBRIDGE (William Blocksidge)

## Moreton Miles

### LIV

Wherever I go, I do no wrong;
My love it burns the same:
So tribes who move the camp along
Carry the guarded flame.

Wherever I go my heart I leave
With my true Love alone:
I gave it as I vowed to give,
For others keeping none.

I ask of her like bushmen told
By travellers of the rain—
Of overlanding mates of old,
If stirring yet or slain.

## Love Redeemed

### XXXIII

The utile canons, the set codes of priests,
The scourge the cloister bred, the unbraced employs,
The fatuous passion that for them desists
And gores itself—for growth are such, or boys?
Are these my senses not the appointed gates
To admit joy to my heart? Am I not human?
Health, sensual joy, these Nature consecrates—
Divine, she made me man, my Love a woman.
Nor yet am I all lust, but know a mean:
My fires have settled from their earlier flood;
My veins grow humbler in the sweat I've seen:
Thus can I love her doubting not my blood.
   More sure in this, my full devotion's done—
   With spirit and sense, by love annealed, at one.

### LXXXII

Who questions if the punctual sun unbars
Earth's pageant, and flings gold upon the east?
If the swift intersessions of high stars
Make beautiful the night, with magic dressed?

Who asks if grass attires this populous earth?
If leaves put forth their flourish upon trees?
If buds on waking sprays have comeliest birth?
And who, that scans, inquires the why of these?
Who questions, tell, man's breath or blood, that comes
We know not whence, yet is, and dates his day?
These, being, have truth beyond all mortal sums
Of much and less, and prompt nor yea or nay.
    A certitude sublime they have, above
    Belief and non-belief. So has our love.


## From *A Wreath*

When tongues will tax me in the public ear,
Or, worse, omit correction for my fault,
When in a wasting grief none standeth near,
Or does so but my poorness to assault,
When flatterers, to pluck me to the bone,
Would break that mail humility has knit,
Or none, my reputation overthrown,
Will tender one up-shouldering word for it,
Or when, the feast done, those assiduous bills
That flocked upon my bread will turn and stab,
O, then I'll mourn the cure for all those ills,
Not found in fortune to be lost in ebb:
I'll mourn thee, friend. But none may put this right;
For Death has sealed thee to perpetual night.

## The Ampler Circumscription

Who, not to trifle with his days or blood,
Would set the seal of purpose on his soul
And gather up his parts to amplitude,
Must turn and dedicate him to a goal.
Then, lest he serve and waste the little light
Or multiply the labour of his load,
So that he come not home before the night,
His feet must know, and straightly tread, the road.
What needeth next? The skill to see what needs,
The power to put impertinence away,
The strength to lift what serveth into deeds—
The auditors of effort, yea and nay.
  The All-wise no offering takes till man hath writ
  The goal, the road, the yea and nay, on it.

## Life's Testament

### II

The brain, the blood, the busy thews
That quickened in the primal ooze
  Support me yet; till ice shall grip
The heart of Earth, no strength they'll lose.

They take my thought, they laugh, they run—
Ere megatherial moons, begun;
  And shall, till they shall drop within
The shattering whirlwinds of the sun.

53

In subtle and essential ways,
Rich with innumerable days,
    To mould, to charge, to impel me still,
Each through my broadest being plays.

They surged to this hour, this transfuse—
The brain, the blood, the busy thews;
    That act of mine the ultimate stars
Shall look on sprang in primal ooze.


## VI

I worshipped, when my veins were fresh,
A glorious fabric of this flesh,
Where all her skill in living lines
And colour (that its form enshrines)
Nature had lavished; in that guess
She had gathered up all loveliness.
All beauty of flesh, and blood, and bone
I saw there: ay, by impulse known,
All the miracle, the power,
Of being had come there to flower.
Each part was perfect in the whole;
The body one was with the soul;
And heedful not, nor having art,
To see them in a several part,
I fell before the flesh, and knew
All spirit in terms of that flesh too.

But blood must wither like the rose:
'Tis wasting as the minute goes:
And flesh, whose shows were wonders high,
Looks piteous when it puts them by.

The shape I had so oft embraced
Was sealed up, and in earth was placed—
And yet not so; for hovering free
Some wraith of it remained with me,
Some subtle influence that brings
A new breath to all beauteous things,
Some sense that in my marrow stirs
To make things mute its ministers.
I fall before the spirit so,
And flesh in terms of spirit know—
The Holy Ghost, the truth that stands
When turned to dust are lips and hands.

## XI

All that I am to Earth belongs:
This Heaven does me violent wrongs.
My fight from fitful loins, my birth,
Are fashioned to the mode of Earth—
Deliberate things, not swiftly given
As some report it falls in Heaven.
This mind is slow to work, this will,
This hand to act them tardier still—
Not dowered with that immediate sense
Deemed in celestial excellence.
True Earth am I, of Earth I'm knit—
O, let me be at peace with it.

## XII

Into ethereal meads,
　Wide azure flowered with stars,
I sped my ravenous soul; it feeds
　Where end nor check the pasture mars.


And, ranging space, defeat
　It found not. But, returned,
It knew that vaulting pleasance sweet—
　Nor health less on this earth it spurned.


Wise thus, it marks, obeys,
　And honours whence it sprung—
The mighty Being that now stays,
　That threw it forth, that takes ere long—


The Being that knows not death,
　The Being that e'er shall be,
Wherein my soul, flesh threading, hath,
　In force, an Earth's eternity.


Yes, Death is dead; and I,
　What now, and what before,
On the vast wave of life go by
　That, reared, shall never reach the shore.

## Sextains

### The Master-Foe

This let who hate me know, and much admire—
They need not toil to mock me, overthrown:
Long have I led who 'gainst myself conspire;
    And for my wreck suffice I can alone.
    Of all that waste me, no thrust as my own
        Is half so dire.

### The Troubled Unquickening

Too beautiful this earth is! Weep I must
    To sense its sureness, and the transience planned
For those I love and me. A doom more just
    (Breath being so swift) had Beauty's violence banned;
    But ah! to know that bliss shall fail not, and
        Our hearts be dust!

## MARY GILMORE

## Dedicatory

### (In Memory of my Father)

I have known many men, and many men
In the quick balance of the mind have weighed.
And even as Abram found his score was ten,
His ten was one, so was my hope betrayed.
But though the tale is told, and fallen spent
Is the first fiction of a great man's name,
Eminent amid the uneminent
He still stands tall; a lonely mark for fame.

So, too, where truth sweeps out time's dusty floor,
I have seen names, long praised, flung out as naught;
And I have seen one, whom the world called poor,
Walking amid the mountains of his thought.

## Of Wonder

Give life its full domain and feed the soul
With wonder; find within a clod a world,
Or, gazing on the rounded dewdrop purled
Upon a leaf, mark how its tiny bowl
Includes the sun; that sun in whose control
The planets run their courses, and the furled
Comet, onward driven, resists what hurled
It downward, outward, to its nether goal.

O, as a child, how often have I stood
And watched a turning furrow, beauty spelled!
That rhythm, that curve of moving earth that felled
In endless seam upon the narrowing rood,
Not e'en the sea itself has me so held,
So to my heart brought full beatitude.

## Boolee, the Bringer of Life

Breast to breast in the whirling,
Palm to palm in the strife,
Boolee spins over the plain,
Boolee, the bringer of life.

Head to the sky uptowering,
Swift-treading foot on the earth,
Held in his loins the tempest,
Boolee comes, giver of birth.

O Boolee, woman and man!
O Boolee, terror and flame!
*Yea* against *Nay* in the night,
Out of the whirlwind I came.

## The Myall in Prison

Lone, lone and lone I stand,
With none to hear my cry.
As the black feet of the night
Go walking down the sky.

The stars they seem but dust
Under those passing feet,
As they, for an instant's space,
Flicker and flame and fleet.

So, on my heart, my grief
Hangs with the weight of doom,
And the black feet of its night
Go walking through my room.

## The Waradgery Tribe

Harried we were, and spent,
  Broken and falling,
Ere as the cranes we went,
  Crying and calling.

59

Summer shall see the bird
　　Backward returning;
Never shall there be heard
　　Those, who went yearning.

Emptied of us the land,
　　Ghostly our going,
Fallen, like spears the hand
　　Dropped in the throwing.

We are the lost who went
　　Like the cranes, crying;
Hunted, lonely, and spent,
　　Broken and dying.


## The Baying Hounds

There was no hunted one
With whom I did not run,
There was no fainting heart
With which I had not part,
The baying hounds bayed me,
Though it was I was free.

Where'er the hard-prest ran,
Was it or beast or man,
As step by step they went
My breath with them was spent;
The very ant I bruised
My heart held interfused.

## *Nationality*

I have grown past hate and bitterness,
I see the world as one:
Yet, though I can no longer hate,
My son is still my son.

All men at God's round table sit
And all men must be fed;
But this loaf in my hand,
This loaf is my son's bread.

## *The Dice were Loaded*

The dice were loaded full and well
The dreadful night that I was born,
The devils danced a tarantelle,
The whimpering plovers fled the corn.

A fox that hunted hungry food
Lifted his head in ravaged cry;
A shadow ran from out the wood,
In after years that shade was I.

I trod the dark mile all alone,
I trod it lone through all the years;
And but the midnight heard my moan,
And but the bitter earth my tears.

I make no plaint, I make no cry,
No back look give to yesterday;
For, where I saw the hazard lie,
I played the game they bid me play.

And now I hang upon a tree,
My lovely body all forlorn;
The loaded dice were thrown for me
Upon the night that I was born.

## The Tenancy

I shall go as my father went,
A thousand plans in his mind,
With something still held unspent
When death lets fall the blind.

I shall go as my mother went,
The ink still wet on the line:
I shall pay no rust as rent
For the house that is mine.

## MARY FULLERTON ('E')

## A Dream

Unwound the long evolvement,
Mankind was fish again,
Gilled in the fluid prison,
And half absolved from pain.

No rapture and no music,
No agonized despair,
No conscience and no dreaming,
No ecstasies of prayer.

No love to flail the pulses,
Nor love that calms the breast,
But cold mechanic motion,
And cold mechanic rest.

Awake, I cried to heaven,
'God, spin thy spiral fast,
Lest, flinching or lethargic,
Man slides into his past.'

## Independence

I resent great instruments
Celebrating my heart's events;
Not for my private joy
Would I a band employ.

I sing my own song
In the high hour;
And when the Dark Power
Bids me be mute,
Yet is a secret lute
Awake in my heart.

## Passivity

Call not on comfort lest she come
With all her helpers sleek and dumb—
Soft ropes that seem as frail as air,
To bind you in a cushioned chair,
With anodyne, and balm, and spell,
To chant of droning ritual.

Traffic with danger, heat, and strain,
Face when it comes the spear of pain:
None that achieve—the bad, the good—
Have sold to comfort, hardihood.

O, flaccid, havened, housed, defended,
Flesh still alive, but *living* ended!
Angels nor devils are of these—
The castaways on velvet ease.

## Lovers

To be unloved brings sweet relief:
The strong adoring eyes
Play the eternal thief
With the soul's fit disguise.

He will not sleep, and let be drawn
The screen of thy soul's ark;
They keep, those lidless eyes,
Thy sanctuary stark.

God, when he made each separate,
Unfashioned his own act,
Giving the lover eyes
So his love's soul be sacked.

To be unloved gives sweet relief;
The one integrity
Of soul is to be lone,
Inviolate, and free.

## Unit

Had Life remained one whole,
Compact of attributes,
Balanced without excess:
Nor men had been, nor brutes.

Had nought been chipped apart,
The fragments found no shapes,
Achieved not temperament:
Men had not been, nor apes.

Undo the forms and lines,
And see the units fall
With prisoned attributes
Back to the primal All.

Oh, gone the tiger's fire,
The blue snake's poison sting,
Each nevermore himself,
But part of everything.

Rob rose of breath and hue,
Diana's limbs unform:
Up, down, and bad and good
Lapped in a pointless norm.

Hope, and desire, and dread,
The mara, and the grapes
Unfeatured, and annulled!
God keep us struggling shapes.

65

F

## Adventure

I heard a halloo in the wood
And went to find who sang;
No elf: but an accoutred wolf
Flashed at me with his fang.

It was a tourney, eye to eye,
Quick staff, and snarling tooth!
Who overcame I cannot tell,
But I emerged forsooth.

My dress and gentle hands were torn;
And, when I reached my door,
There on the lintel was a name
That was not there before.

And now he does not come again,
Who got no welcome in,
But thinking on his signature
I know the might have been.

With life unanswered, heart secure,
I should have lived, and died—
Unknown the mighty Terrible,
Splendid and tawny-eyed.

## RODERIC QUINN

### *The Fisher*

All night a noise of leaping fish
Went round the bay,
And up and down the shallow sands
Sang waters at their play.

The mangroves drooped on salty creeks,
And through the dark,
Making a pale patch in the deep,
Gleamed, as it swam, a shark.

In streaks and twists of sudden fire
Among the reeds
The bream went by, and where they passed
The bubbles shone like beads.

All night the full deep drinking-song
Of nature stirred,
And nought beside, save leaping fish
And some forlorn night-bird.

No lost wind wandered down the hills
To tell of wide
Wild waterways; on velvet moved
The silky, sucking tide.

Deep down there sloped in shadowy mass
A giant hill;
And midway, mirrored in the tide,
The stars burned large and still.

The fisher, dreaming on the rocks,
Heard Nature say
Strange secret things that none may hear
Upon the beaten way

And whisperings and wonder stirred,
And hopes and fears,
And sadness touched his heart, and filled
His eyes with star-stained tears:

And so, thrilled through with joy and love
And sweet distress,
He stood entranced, enchained by her
Full-breasted loveliness.


## JAMES DEVANEY

### Mortality

The lone watch of the moon over mountains old.
Night that is never silent, and none to hark.
Down in the inky pool a fish leaps
With splash of silver light in the liquid dark.

I walk the unknown ways of a foreign land.
The close reeds whisper their secrecies,
And hidden water tunes—earth's oldest voice.
What alien waif is mind among mindless these?

Old, old, everything here is old.
Life the intruder but so briefly stays,
And man the dreamer—soon old changeless time
Will grass his ways.

Fold him, spade him away. Where are they now,
The high courage and love, the laboured store?
Down in the inky pool a fish leapt—
Life is no more.

## Winter Westerlies

Leaning against the wind across the paddock ways
Comes Dan home with forward stoop like a man bent and old,
Clashes the door in haste as one pursued: 'By Christ it's cold!'
And crooks his fingers to the blaze.

We do not live these days, but each exhausting day
Unnerved we numbly wait return of life, and must abide
The wind, the still beleaguering wind; all voices else outside
Imperiously it has blown away.

Over the bronze-brown paddocks the grass is bowed flat down;
Along the birdless creek a cold malevolence has passed;
A forlorn sparrow clings on the fence against the icy blast,
His soft breast-feathers loosely blown.

We watch the saplings buffeted without repose,
Their foliage all on one side, plunging without rest,
Stems leaning all one way from the assailing west,
Bending as backs cower from blows.

The hunched cattle no longer feeding dejected stand
With dumb endurance, tails to the flogging wind hour after
    hour;
From some far frozen hell of winds a blind and soulless power
Invades and harries all the land.

The wind! The wind! It fumbles at the fastened panes,
Fills and possesses all, a tyranny without control;
Ceaseless, changeless, malign, searching into the very soul
The rushing desolation reigns.

HUGH McCRAE

## Colombine

Exit the ribald clown
   Enter like bubbling wine,
Lighter than thistledown,
   Sweet little Colombine.

      Whisht! and behold the game,
         Long eyes and pointed chin
      Paler than candleflame,
         At her feet Harlequin.

Look how their shadows run,
   Swift as she flies from him!—
Moths in the morning sun,
   Out of a garden dim.

      Faint through the fluttering
         Fall of a flute divine,
      Softly the 'cellos sing
         *'Colombine, Colombine.'*

Softly the 'cellos sing:
   *'Colombine'* . . .
   *'Colombine'* . . .

## *June Morning*

The twisted apple, with rain and magian fire
Caught in its branches from the early dawn,
I, from my bed, through the fogged pane see, and desire
Of its sharp sweetness, something: green the lawn
And stiff with pointed spears of daffodils run wild;
The sluggard sun draws the drowned Daphne back to life—
And all the drowsy doves, brown sparrows, husband, wife,
Are stirring on the housetops—child to early child
Coo-eeing and calling; blind windows open eyes. . .
And in the air the bitter fragrance floats
Of someone's gardener's pipe; I will arise
And in the stinging shower forget gold motes,
Thick pillows, blankets, books; travel the wholesome road
And give my body to the sun.

## *Enigma*

I watch her fingers where they prance
    Like little naked women, tango-mad,
Along the keys, a cup-shot dance—
    Music, who'll say, more joyous or more sad?

A mystery . . . but not so strange
    As she. Enigma is her pretty name;
And though she smiles, her veiled eyes range
    Through tears of melancholy and shame.

She laughs and weeps. . . . Is it because
    Only tonight she gave herself to me?
The new bud frightened to be glad. . . .
    The child's first vision of the insatiate sea.

71

## *Song of the Rain*

Night,
    And the yellow pleasure of candlelight . . .
    Old brown books and the kind fine face of the clock
    Fogged in the veils of the fire; its cuddling tock.

The cat
    Greening her eyes on the flame-litten mat;
    Wickedly wakeful, she yawns at the rain
    Bending the roses over the pane.
    And a bird in my heart begins to sing
    Over and over the same sweet thing.

    'Safe in the house with my boyhood's love,
    And our children asleep in the attic above.'

## *Ambuscade*

Or the black centaurs, statuesquely still,
Whose moving eyes devour the snuffling mares,
And watch with baneful rage their nervous strides
Whip the dark river white, lest unawares
Some danger seize them. . . . Statuesquely still,
Behind the waving trellises of cane,
The centaurs feel their hearts (besieged with blood)
Stagger like anvils when the sled-blows rain
Shower on shower in persistent flood. . . .

Now Cornus, he, the oldest of the group,
With many wounds, strong arms, and clay-rolled hair,
Coughs for a signal to his dreadful troop,
And springs, wide-fingered, from the crackling lair.

72

Loudly the victims neigh, they thrash the stream,
They tear their foemen's beards with frothy teeth,
And fill the banks with sparkling spires of steam
That heavenward roll in one tumultuous wreath.

Within the branches of an ancient oak,
A Mother-Satyr, sleeping with her young,
Smit by a sudden stone, upbraids the stroke,
Then turns to see from whence it has been flung.
Scarce does she view the cursed Centaur-pack,
Than, standing clear, she blows a whistle shrill,
Which, like an echo, straight comes flying back
Louder and louder down the empty hill.
A roar of hooves, a lightning-view of eyes
Redder than fire, of long, straight whistling manes,
Stiff crests, and tails drawn out against the skies,
Of angry nostrils webbed with leaping veins,
The stallions come . . .

## Morning

The grand red sun has glistened in,
And through the curtain I can see
His disc upon the steeple-pin
(Just touching) of St Anthony.

The night mist on the window flows
In long, wet channels down the pane,
And from the distance slowly grows
The rattle of a country train.

73

But here, in this disordered room,
The dusty motes stand motionless
Above the glasses in the gloom
That rang last night with merriness.

A spotted spider walks between
The long white fingers of her glove,
Like feathers opened out, to preen,
By some proud thoughtless lady-dove.

Her little sober churchy hat,
Her month-old summer muslin gown,
The short half-stays I marvelled at—
A Frenchman's symphony in brown—

(These, set within a chair, are hid;
A mountain heaped up carelessly—
Sweets hiding other sweets amid
A cataract of lingerie.)

And she herself, still breathing sound,
Her passive eyes fast-closed in sleep,
Waits weary, in her bed, the round
Black Fortune means that she should keep.

Ah frail and sadly beautiful—
Above us in the blue-breast sky
Those stars at dusk most visible
Are now lost treasures to the eye.

And you, a mortal star on earth,
Perhaps, like that bright sisterhood,
So fair by night, may, at the birth
Of Day, be no more where you stood.

74

And so (that I may see you yet
As when across the lighted Place
Your beauty caught me in its net
And held me by its sovran grace)

I'll leave you softly to yourself
Before a second quarter-chime,
With this memento on the shelf
Until the purple evening time.

Sleep on—your glossy hair unrolled
Burns in my fingers, and I see
A ghostly lover in its gold
Look backward mockingly at me . . .

Another, and another—lo!
Each tress reveals a satyr-face . . .
But I must stop this play and go—
Or choke you with your pillow-lace!

## The End of Desire

A flooded fold of sarcenet
Against her slender body sank,
Death-black, and beaded all with jet
Across the pleasures of her flank.

The incense of a holy bowl
Flowed round her knees, till it did seem
That she was standing on the shore
Of some forbidden sunlit stream.

A little gong, far through the wall,
Complained like one deep sorrowing,
And from the arras I saw fall
The woven swallow fluttering;

While o'er the room there swam the breath
Of roses on a trellised tree;
Loose ladies in pretended death
Of sweet abandon to the bee.

Flames filled the hollows of my hands;
Red blood rushed, hammering, round my heart,
Like mighty sleds when anvil bands
Gape out, and from their holdings start.

No peace had I, and knew not where
To find a solace that would kill
This pain of flesh so hard to bear,
This sin of soul against the will.

But ever yet mine eyes would seek
That golden woman built for love,
Whose either breast displayed the beak
Through pouted plumes, of Venus' dove.

Her heavy hair, as smoke blown down
Athwart the fields of plenteousness;
Her folded lips, her placid frown,
Her insolence of nakedness.

I took her closely, but while yet
I trembled, vassal to my lust,
Lo!—Nothing but some sarcenet
Deep-buried in a pile of dust.

## Fragment

As if stone Cæsar shook
His staff across the wet
Black passages, and took
With marble eyes a yet
Unconquered gaze of Rome;
Marked how the cypress boughs
Stood thick about his home
As when he bent his brows
Three centuries before
Across some Gordian knot
His civic business wore—
*Hic jacet* the whole lot.

What hammer fell? And whose
The crushed white paper skull
Mixed in the side-bank ooze
Of mighty Tiber . . . Dull
The mind and hand that first
Wrought sparth and sinker-blade,
Knobbed clubs and spikes to burst
The fairy spirit from the shade
He entered in, when through a mesh
Of aching tissues, blood to blood,
And flesh on softly folding flesh,
Man with his woman made a flood
Of kings and weavers, so the world
Might fling about in sunny ways,
Some to the hunt, and some, up-curled,
Stung silent in the martyr's blaze.

77

LEONARD MANN

## *The Earth*

Minute made visible and heard,
  Fact born of space by lust of time,
The aftermath of the first word,
  Mote dried from a drift of slime:

Earth, 'tis enough to know but this,
  You give such beauty to our eyes
And all our senses, here love is
  And the dream-stuff of Paradise.

Your rise in night and your decline
  Sentries nor scientists behold,
No lovers pray of you divine
  Heat for a loved one's heart grown cold.

Yet in illimitable law
  Guessed at by symbols, you may be
Lovely as Venus whom you saw
  This night above your darkening sea.

And where a world has come alive
  May not your littleness be host,
Food of the spirit, the soul's hive,
  Home and haven of Holy Ghost?

## Meditation in Winter

Inside the house I sit alone.
The frost will form upon the grass
In meagre paddocks and thin ice
Will glaze the mud and puddles soon.
I see beyond the window-glass
The trees are polished by the moon.

And smoking by the burning log
I grin and wonder how soon I
Will stiffen in death's frost, will lie
Beyond sun's help which, when the fog
Lifts towards next noon, will liquefy
The grass to ripple like a flag.

Believing an escape I made
I left the city yesterday.
Death's grab just missed me on the way.
We passed each other on the road
When the full bus brushed on a dray
That lumbered with a firewood load.

Escape! There is a city in
The fragile fabric of my skull,
This mind, my body's capital,
Whose people sometimes somehow win
To visions strange and beautiful
That fade like dreams before the sun.

Yet like an airman in the night
I see that secret city break
Into a maze of lights and wake
When morning drowns those stars in light,
All gilded and with towers that shake
With bells and tall spires jubilate.

And then know a dead stillness come
And in thick scales the roofs are spread
Upon earth's skin as if some dread
Disease and over it a scum
Of smoke the foul factories feed
Like boils bursting a squalid slum.

There might a river silver run
Through satined shadows and as clear
As in the mountains over there
And shot through long leaves by the sun,
A stream of poetry and lovelier
Than flowed the crystal Helicon.

O if this I could now rebuild
That city to a better plan,
As beautiful as that begun
In dream and then left unfulfilled
When art must put the dream upon
The substance of a real world.

Rebuild that city beautiful,
Rebuild, rebuild it many times,
That city loved in hopes and dreams,
Until its toiling peoples shall
Be changed and so itself redeems
Them for the full life of the soul.

A change strikes on the window-glass:
The wind is risen and the moon
Is lost in heaviest cloud and soon,
I know, the hunched and running grass
Will feel the lashes of the rain
Ere of the sun it comfort has.

## E. G. MOLL

### Beware the Cuckoo

Beware the cuckoo, though she bring
Authentic tidings of the spring.
And though her voice among the trees
Transport you to the Hebrides!

I saw her come one sunny day,
And pause awhile and fly away,
And I knew where she took her rest
There was a honeyeater's nest.

Later I came again and found
Three dead fledglings on the ground,
And red ants busy in a throng
At throats that had been made for song.

But in the low nest in the tree
The cuckoo chick sat cosily,
And seemed to my unhappy sight
A grey and monstrous appetite.

Beware the cuckoo! By what name
You call her, she is still the same.
And, if you must admire her art,
Keep a wing over your heart.

81

G

## On Having Grown Old

Now are those peaks unscalable sierras
Against a darkening sky. I may not climb,
Sure of my skill, contemptuous of errors,
Their crags as gaily as once upon a time.
To reach those heights, now, even were I able,
Were but to push a faltering heart too far
And to be laid out at last on a stone table
Bare to the gaze of a mortician star.

>       No, never again! But from the dull plain counting,
>       Before dark blot them, every hazardous peak,
>       I'll let my eyes leap in a swift upmounting
>       To what I knew, and having known, still seek;
>       Then, on my slab, while stars put on their white
>       Uniforms, yield myself to absolute night.

## KENNETH SLESSOR

### Earth-Visitors

There were strange riders once, came gusting down
Cloaked in dark furs, with faces grave and sweet,
And white as air. None knew them, they were strangers—
Princes gone feasting, barons with gipsy eyes
And names that rang like viols—perchance, who knows,
Kings of old Tartary, forgotten, swept from Asia,
Blown on raven chargers across the world,
For ever smiling sadly in their beards
   And stamping abruptly into courtyards at midnight.

Post-boys would run, lanterns hang frostily, horses fume,
The strangers wake the Inn. Men, staring outside
Past watery glass, thick panes, could watch them eat,
Dyed with gold vapours in the candleflame,
Clapping their gloves, and stuck with crusted stones,
Their garments foreign, their talk a strange tongue,
    But sweet as pineapple—it was Archdukes, they must be.


In daylight, nothing; only their prints remained
Bitten in snow. They'd gone, no one knew where,
Or when, or by what road—no one could guess—
None but some sleepy girls, half tangled in dreams,
Mixing up miracle and desire; laughing, at first,
Then staring with bright eyes at their beds, opening their lips,
Plucking a crushed gold feather in their fingers,
And laughing again, eyes closed. But one remembered,
Between strange kisses and cambric, in the dark,
That unearthly beard had lifted . . . 'Your name, child?'
'Sophia, sir—and what to call your grace?'
    Like a bubble of gilt, he had laughed 'Mercury!'


It is long now since great daemons walked on earth,
Staining with wild radiance a country bed,
And leaving only a confusion of sharp dreams
To vex a farm-girl—that, and perhaps a feather,
Some thread of the Cloth of Gold, a scale of metal,
Caught in her hair. The unpastured Gods have gone,
They are above those fiery-coasted clouds
Floating like fins of stone in the burnt air,
And earth is only a troubled thought to them
That sometimes drifts like wind across the bodies
    Of the sky's women.

There is one yet comes knocking in the night,
The drums of sweet conspiracy on the pane,
When darkness has arched his hands over the bush
And Springwood steams with dew, and the stars look down
On that one lonely chamber . . .
She is there suddenly, lit by no torch or moon,
But by the shining of her naked body.
Her breasts are berries broken in snow; her hair
Blows in a gold rain over and over them.
She flings her kisses like warm guineas of love,
    And when she walks, the stars walk with her above.

She knocks. The door swings open, shuts again.
'Your name, child?'
    A thousand birds cry 'Venus!'


## Stars

'These are the floating berries of the night,
   They drop their harvest in dark alleys down,
   Softly far down on groves of Venus, or on a little town
Forgotten at the world's edge—and O, their light
Unlocks all closed things, eyes and mouths, and drifts
   Quietly over kisses in a golden rain,
Drowning their flight, till suddenly the Cyprian lifts
   Her small, white face to the moon, then hides again.

'They are the warm candles of beauty, hung in blessing on
    high,
   Poised like bright comrades on boughs of night above;
They are the link-boys of Queen Venus, running out of the sky,
   Spilling their friendly radiance on all her ways of love.

'Should the girl's eyes be lit with swimming fire,
　　O do not kiss it away, it is a star, a star!'
　So cried the passionate poet to his great, romantic guitar.

But I was beating off the stars, gazing, not rhyming.
　　I saw the bottomless, black cups of space
Between their clusters, and the planets climbing
　　Dizzily in sick airs, and desired to hide my face.
But I could not escape those tunnels of nothingness,
　　The cracks in the spinning Cross, nor hold my brain
From rushing for ever down that terrible lane,
　　Infinity's trapdoor, eternal and merciless.

## Five Visions of Captain Cook

### I

Cook was a captain of the Admiralty
When sea-captains had the evil eye,
Or should have, what with beating krakens off
And casting nativities of ships;
Cook was a captain of the powder-days
When captains, you might have said, if you had been
Fixed by their glittering stare, half-down the side,
Or gaping at them up companionways,
Were more like warlocks than a humble man—
And men were humble then who gazed at them,
Poor horn-eyed sailors, bullied by devils' fists
Of wind or water, or the want of both,
Childlike and trusting, filled with eager trust—
Cook was a captain of the sailing days
When sea-captains were kings like this,
Not cold executives of company-rules

Cracking their boilers for a dividend
Or bidding their engineers go wink
At bells and telegraphs, so plates would hold
Another pound. Those captains drove their ships
By their own blood, no laws of schoolbook steam,
Till yards were sprung, and masts went overboard—
Daemons in periwigs, doling magic out,
Who read fair alphabets in stars
Where humbler men found but a mess of sparks,
Who steered their crews by mysteries
And strange, half-dreadful sortilege with books,
Used medicines that only gods could know
The sense of, but sailors drank
In simple faith. That was the captain
Cook was when he came to the Coral Sea
And chose a passage into the dark.

How many mariners had made that choice
Paused on the brink of mystery! 'Choose now!'
The winds roared, blowing home, blowing home,
Over the Coral Sea. 'Choose now!' the trades
Cried once to Tasman, throwing him for choice
Their teeth or shoulders, and the Dutchman chose
The wind's way, turning north. 'Choose, Bougainville!'
The wind cried once, and Bougainville had heard
The voice of God calling him prudently
Out of a dead lee shore, and chose the north,
The wind's way. So, too, Cook made choice,
Over the brink, into the devil's mouth,
With four months' food, and sailors wild with dreams
Of English beer, the smoking barns of home.
So Cook made choice, so Cook sailed westabout,
So men write poems in Australia.

*links with the past are not to be ashamed of.*

## II

Flowers turned to stone! Not all the botany
Of Joseph Banks, hung pensive in a porthole,
Could find the Latin for this loveliness,
Could put the Barrier Reef in a glass box
Tagged by the horrid Gorgon squint
Of horticulture. Stone turned to flowers
It seemed—you'd snap a crystal twig,
One petal even of the water-garden,
And have it dying like a cherry-bough.

They'd sailed all day outside a coral hedge,
And half the night. Cook sailed at night,
Let there be reefs a fathom from the keel
And empty charts. The sailors didn't ask,
Nor Joseph Banks. Who cared? It was the spell
Of Cook that lulled them, bade them turn below,
Kick off their sea-boots, puff themselves to sleep,
Though there were more shoals outside
Than teeth in a shark's head. Cook snored loudest himself.

One day, a morning of light airs and calms,
They slid towards a reef that would have knifed
Their boards to mash, and murdered every man.
So close it sucked them, one wave shook their keel,
The next blew past the coral. Three officers,
In gilt and buttons, languidly on deck
Pointed their sextants at the sun. One yawned,
One held a pencil, one put eye to lens;
Three very peaceful English mariners
Taking their sights for longitude.
I've never heard
Of sailors aching for the longitude

Of shipwrecks before or since. It was the spell
Of Cook did this, the phylacteries of Cook.
Men who ride broomsticks with a mesmerist
Mock the typhoon. So, too, it was with Cook.

### III

Two chronometers the captain had,
One by Arnold that ran like mad,
One by Kendal in a walnut case,
Poor devoted creature with a hangdog face.

*Greenwich and local times → contrast*

Arnold always hurried with a crazed click-click
Dancing over Greenwich like a lunatic,
Kendal panted faithfully his watch-dog beat,
Climbing out of Yesterday with sticky little feet.

Arnold choked with appetite to wolf up time,
Madly round the numerals his hands would climb,
His cogs rushed over and his wheels ran miles,
Dragging Captain Cook to the Sandwich Isles.

But Kendal dawdled in the tombstoned past,
With a sentimental prejudice to going fast,
And he thought very often of a haberdasher's door
And a yellow-haired boy who would knock no more.

All through the night-time, clock talked to clock,
In the captain's cabin, tock-tock-tock,
One ticked fast and one ticked slow,
And Time went over them a hundred years ago.

### IV

Sometimes the god would fold his wings
And, stone of Caesars turned to flesh
Talk of the most important things
That serious-minded midshipmen could wish,

Of plantains, and the lack of rum,
Or spearing sea-cows—things like this
That hungry schoolboys, five days dumb,
In jolly-boats are wonted to discuss.

What midshipman would pause to mourn
The sun that beat about his ears,
Or curse the tide, if he could horn
His fists by tugging on those lumbering oars?

Let rum-tanned mariners prefer
To hug the weather-side of yards;
'Cats to catch mice' before they purr,
Those were the captain's enigmatic words.

Here, in this jolly-boat they graced,
Were food and freedom, wind and storm,
While, fowling-piece across his waist,
Cook mapped the coast, with one eye cocked for game.

### V

After the candles had gone out, and those
Who listened had gone out, and a last wave
Of chimney-haloes caked their smoky rings
Like fish-scales on the ceiling, a Yellow Sea
Of swimming circles, the old man,

*reminiscing*

Old Captain-in-the-Corner, drank his rum
With friendly gestures to four chairs. They stood
Empty, still warm from haunches, with rubbed nails
And leather glazed, like agèd serving-men
Feeding a king's delight, the sticky, drugged
Sweet agony of habitual anecdotes.
But these, his chairs, could bear an old man's tongue,
Sleep when he slept, be flattering when he woke,
And wink to hear the same eternal name
From lips new-dipped in rum.

'Then Captain Cook,
I heard him, told them they could go
If so they chose, but he would get them back,
Dead or alive, he'd have them,'
The old man screeched, half-thinking to hear 'Cook!
Cook again! Cook! It's other cooks he'll need,
Cooks who can bake a dinner out of pence,
That's what he lives on, talks on, half-a-crown
A day, and sits there full of Cook.
Who'd do your cooking now, I'd like to ask,
If someone didn't grind her bones away?
But that's the truth, six children and half-a-crown
A day, and a man gone daft with Cook.'

That was his wife,
Elizabeth, a noble wife but brisk,
Who lived in a present full of kitchen-fumes
And had no past. He had not seen her
For seven years, being blind, and that of course
Was why he'd had to strike a deal with chairs,
Not knowing when those who chafed them had gone to sleep
Or stolen away. Darkness and empty chairs,

This was the port that Alexander Home
Had come to with his useless cutlass-wounds
And tales of Cook, and half-a-crown a day—
This was the creek he'd run his timbers to,
Where grateful countrymen repaid his wounds
At half-a-crown a day. Too good, too good,
This eloquent offering of birdcages
To gulls, and Greenwich Hospital to Cook,
Britannia's mission to the sea-fowl.

It was not blindness picked his flesh away,
Nor want of sight made penny-blank the eyes
Of Captain Home, but that he lived like this
In one place, and gazed elsewhere. His body moved
In Scotland, but his eyes were dazzle-full
Of skies and water farther round the world—
Air soaked with blue, so thick it dripped like snow
On spice-tree boughs, and water diamond-green,
Beaches wind-glittering with crumbs of gilt,
And birds more scarlet than a duchy's seal
That had come whistling long ago, and far
Away. His body had gone back,
Here it sat drinking rum in Berwickshire,
But not his eyes—they were left floating there
Half-round the earth, blinking at beaches milked
By suck-mouth tides, foaming with ropes of bubbles
And huge half-moons of surf. Thus it had been
When Cook was carried on a sailor's back,
Vengeance in a cocked hat, to claim his price,
A prince in barter for a longboat.
And then the trumpery springs of fate—a stone,
A musket-shot, a round of gunpowder,
And puzzled animals, killing they knew not what

Or why, but killing . . . the surge of goatish flanks
Armoured in feathers, like cruel birds:
Wild, childish faces, killing; a moment seen,
Marines with crimson coats and puffs of smoke
Toppling face down; and a knife of English iron,
Forged aboard ship, that had been changed for pigs,
Given back to Cook between the shoulder-blades.
There he had dropped, and the old floundering sea,
The old, fumbling, witless lover-enemy,
Had taken his breath, last office of salt water.

*Sea as lover/enemy*

Cook died. The body of Alexander Home
Flowed round the world and back again, with eyes
Marooned already, and came to English coasts,
The vague ancestral darknesses of home,
Seeing them faintly through a glass of gold,
Dim fog-shapes, ghosted like the ribs of trees
Against his blazing waters and blue air.
But soon they faded, and there was nothing left,
Only the sugar-cane and the wild granaries
Of sand, and palm-trees and the flying blood
Of cardinal-birds; and putting out one hand
Tremulously in the direction of the beach,
He felt a chair in Scotland. And sat down.

*even in retirement he remembers*

## Crow Country

Gutted of station, noise alone,
The crow's voice trembles down the sky
As if this nitrous flange of stone
Wept suddenly with such a cry;

As if the rock found lips to sigh,
The riven earth a mouth to moan;
But we that hear them, stumbling by,
Confuse their torments with our own.

Over the huge abraded rind,
Crow-countries graped with dung, we go,
Past gullies that no longer flow
And wells that nobody can find,
Lashed by the screaming of the crow,
Stabbed by the needles of the mind.

## Gulliver

I'll kick your walls to bits, I'll die scratching a tunnel,
If you'll give me a wall, if you'll give me simple stone,
If you'll do me the honour of a dungeon—
Anything but this tyranny of sinews.
Lashed with a hundred ropes of nerve and bone
I lie, poor helpless Gulliver,
In a twopenny dock for the want of a penny,
Tied up with stuff too cheap, and strings too many.
One chain is usually sufficient for a cur.

Hair over hair, I pick my cables loose,
But still the ridiculous manacles confine me.
I snap them, swollen with sobbing. What's the use?
One hair I break, ten thousand hairs entwine me.
Love, hunger, drunkenness, neuralgia, debt,
Cold weather, hot weather, sleep and age—
If I could only unloose their spongy fingers,
I'd have a chance yet, slip through the cage.
But who ever heard of a cage of hairs?
You can't scrape tunnels in a net.

93

If you'd give me a chain, if you'd give me honest iron,
If you'd graciously give me a turnkey,
I could break my teeth on a chain, I could bite through metal,
But what can you do with hairs?
For God's sake, call the hangman.

## Sleep

Do you give yourself to me utterly,
    Body and no-body, flesh and no-flesh,
Not as a fugitive, blindly or bitterly,
    But as a child might, with no other wish?
*Yes, utterly.*

Then I shall bear you down my estuary,
Carry you and ferry you to burial mysteriously,
Take you and receive you,
Consume you, engulf you,
In the huge cave, my belly, lave you
With huger waves continually.

And you shall cling and clamber there
And slumber there, in that dumb chamber,
Beat with my blood's beat, hear my heart move
Blindly in bones that ride above you,
Delve in my flesh, dissolved and bedded,
Through viewless valves embodied so—

Till daylight, the expulsion and awakening,
    The riving and the driving forth,
Life with remorseless forceps beckoning—
    Pangs and betrayal of harsh birth.

94

## Five Bells

*Time that is moved by little fidget wheels*
*Is not my Time, the flood that does not flow.*
*Between the double and the single bell*
*Of a ship's hour, between a round of bells*
*From the dark warship riding there below,*
*I have lived many lives, and this one life*
*Of Joe, long dead, who lives between five bells.*

Deep and dissolving verticals of light
Ferry the falls of moonshine down. Five bells
Coldly rung out in a machine's voice. Night and water
Pour to one rip of darkness, the Harbour floats
In air, the Cross hangs upside-down in water.

Why do I think of you, dead man, why thieve
These profitless lodgings from the flukes of thought
Anchored in Time? You have gone from earth,
Gone even from the meaning of a name;
Yet something's there, yet something forms its lips
And hits and cries against the ports of space,
Beating their sides to make its fury heard.

Are you shouting at me, dead man, squeezing your face
In agonies of speech on speechless panes?
Cry louder, beat the windows, bawl your name!

But I hear nothing, nothing . . . only bells,
Five bells, the bumpkin calculus of Time.
Your echoes die, your voice is dowsed by Life,
There's not a mouth can fly the pygmy strait—
Nothing except the memory of some bones

Long shoved away, and sucked away, in mud;
And unimportant things you might have done,
Or once I thought you did; but you forgot,
And all have now forgotten—looks and words
And slops of beer; your coat with buttons off,
Your gaunt chin and pricked eye, and raging tales
Of Irish kings and English perfidy,
And dirtier perfidy of publicans
Groaning to God from Darlinghurst.

*Five bells.*

Then I saw the road, I heard the thunder
Tumble, and felt the talons of the rain
The night we came to Moorebank in slab-dark,
So dark you bore no body, had no face,
But a sheer voice that rattled out of air
(As now you'd cry if I could break the glass),
A voice that spoke beside me in the bush,
Loud for a breath or bitten off by wind,
Of Milton, melons and the Rights of Man,
And blowing flutes, and how Tahitian girls
Are brown and angry-tongued, and Sydney girls
Are white and angry-tongued, or so you'd found.
But all I heard was words that didn't join,
So Milton became melons, melons girls,
And fifty mouths, it seemed, were out that night,
And in each tree an Ear was bending down,
Or something had just run, gone behind grass,
When, blank and bone-white, like a maniac's thought,
The naphtha-flash of lightning slit the sky,
Knifing the dark with deathly photographs.
There's not so many with so poor a purse

Or fierce a need, must fare by night like that,
Five miles in darkness on a country track,
But when you do, that's what you think.

*Five bells.*


In Melbourne, your appetite had gone,
Your angers too; they had been leeched away
By the soft archery of summer rains
And the sponge-paws of wetness, the slow damp
That stuck the leaves of living, snailed the mind,
And showed your bones, that had been sharp with rage,
The sodden ecstasies of rectitude.
I thought of what you'd written in faint ink,
Your journal with the sawn-off lock, that stayed behind
With other things you left, all without use,
And without meaning now, except a sign
That someone had been living who now was dead:
'At Labassa. Room 6 × 8
On top of the tower; because of this, very dark
And cold in winter. Everything has been stowed
Into this room—500 books all shapes
And colours, dealt across the floor
And over sills and on the laps of chairs;
Guns, photoes of many differant things
And differant curioes that I obtained . . .'


In Sydney, by the spent aquarium-flare
Of penny gaslight on pink wallpaper,
We argued about blowing up the world,
But you were living backward, so each night
You crept a moment closer to the breast,
And they were living, all of them, those frames
And shapes of flesh that had perplexed your youth,

97

And most your father, the old man gone blind,
With fingers always round a fiddle's neck,
That graveyard mason whose fair monuments
And tablets cut with dreams of piety
Rest on the bosoms of a thousand men
Staked bone by bone, in quiet astonishment
At cargoes they had never thought to bear,
These funeral-cakes of sweet and sculptured stone.

Where have you gone? The tide is over you,
The turn of midnight water's over you,
As Time is over you, and mystery,
And memory, the flood that does not flow.
You have no suburb, like those easier dead
In private berths of dissolution laid—
The tide goes over, the waves ride over you
And let their shadows down like shining hair,
But they are Water; and the sea-pinks bend
Like lilies in your teeth, but they are Weed;
And you are only part of an Idea.
I felt the wet push its black thumb-balls in,
The night you died, I felt your eardrums crack,
And the short agony, the longer dream,
The Nothing that was neither long nor short;
But I was bound, and could not go that way,
But I was blind, and could not feel your hand.
If I could find an answer, could only find
Your meaning, or could say why you were here
Who now are gone, what purpose gave you breath
Or seized it back, might I not hear your voice?

I looked out of my window in the dark
At waves with diamond quills and combs of light

*triumph of
the environment*

That arched their mackerel-backs and smacked the sand
In the moon's drench, that straight enormous glaze,
And ships far off asleep, and Harbour-buoys
Tossing their fireballs wearily each to each,
And tried to hear your voice, but all I heard
Was a boat's whistle, and the scraping squeal
Of seabirds' voices far away, and bells,
Five bells. Five bells coldly ringing out.

*Five bells.*


# Beach Burial

Softly and humbly to the gulf of Arabs
The convoys of dead sailors come;
At night they sway and wander in the waters far under,
But morning rolls them in the foam.

Between the sob and clubbing of the gunfire
Someone, it seems, has time for this,
To pluck them from the shallows and bury them in burrows
And tread the sand upon their nakedness;

And each cross, the driven stake of tide-wood,
Bears the last signature of men,
Written with such perplexity, with such bewildered pity,
The words choke as they begin—

'*Unknown seaman*'—the ghostly pencil
Wavers and fades, the purple drips,
The breath of the wet season has washed their inscriptions
As blue as drowned men's lips,

Dead seamen, gone in search of the same landfall,
Whether as enemies they fought,
Or fought with us, or neither; the sand joins them together,
Enlisted on the other front.

## JOHN THOMPSON

### Letter to a Friend

Dear George,

       At last the blowfly's buzz retreats,
The sweats of summer fade, the autumn heats
Withdraw their torrid mantle. Winter comes.
No more the sharp mosquito whines and hums
Around the sleepers in their burning bed.
Keen winter nips them on the nose instead.
The sun, the regular soldier of the sky,
No longer flays us with his angry eye,
For mists and frosts and wild wet winds at last
Return—like friends recovered from the past.

One friend's away. What reason, what unreason,
Drives you to shun this retrospective season?
You should be here to pledge me drink for drink,
When, by my fire, into my chair I sink:
To bandy joke for joke, while stormy night
Rampages, rages, roars with all his might,
Whips the forsaken streets with whirling rains,
Rattles the doors, and shakes the window-panes.

You should be with me, while the claret flows,
Twisting and stroking your mustachios,
And mingling memories to revive the fun
Of all that we have seen and been and done.


Ah, George, a world of girls has learnt the trick
Since you and I first guttered at the wick;
A world of boys, ruled by unruly glands,
Swaggers and swells in ostentatious stands.
Let them. For us the ageing interchange
Of slack for tense, of ordinary for strange,
Offers the promise of approaching ease
Where actions fade to reminiscences.
Few have we known who tasted more than us
Folly's extremes or passion's overplus;
Few, too, who braved with such delightful strife
The incalculable cataract of life
To reach the central torrent, the clear sweep
Of confident waters channelling smooth and deep
Beyond all idle pools and foolish froth.


One truth we firmly hold, upon my oath,
(Not only for ourselves, for others too)
That each should do as he desires to do.
Inland and northward (would that you were here)
Nature walks with a blossom at each ear;
So, though my fire be snug, my cellar rich,
I cannot blame you for your restless itch.
Old though you be in every chromosome,
Go on, go further; for the more you roam
The finer fables you will bring back home.

Where are you drinking now, with rosy face?
In what unmapped or half-forgotten place
Plotting a detour of a thousand miles
To hunt for folk-songs or for crocodiles?
Upon what mangrove beach or coral cay
Animal-naked all the livelong day?
Above what mountain, borne on silver wings,
Flying your thirst to Broome or Alice Springs?

Mean minds, though they may cage the hawk or fox,
Cannot keep radium in a cardboard box;
They cannot strap up gales or gag the thunder
Or screw down clamps to hold an earthquake under;
Much less can they emasculate or kill
Man's giant affection, his titanic will,
Or the huge Joy that drives him up the cliffs
Of the most wild Perhapses and dangerous Ifs.
Dullness and Hatred, meeting no resistance,
Lose themselves in emptiness and distance,
But vital Gusto, bursting from duress,
Prospers in unrestraint and boundlessness.

Rejoice, dear George, in freedom. I admit
That, were you here, we'd talk with better wit
Of what we wish for than of what we did,
Long since, in bright Papeete or Madrid.
Above my roof the wrathy weather rolls;
Within, red orchids bloom among the coals.
Down the wet street belated taxis hiss;
Within, is warmth. Only yourself I miss.
Were I with you, how rousing it would be,
Over some murmuring moonlit tropic sea,

To steer for scenes unvisited before,
Cuzco, Mauritius, Bangkok, Travancore.
Enough, enough! Don't tempt me any more!
Loth as yourself the tether's length to learn,
I drink (from this full glass) to your return.

## ROBERT D. FITZGERALD

### From *Copernicus*

The cock that crowed this dawn up, heard
along the east an earlier call
as through sunk acres bird by bird
till imminent upon sleep's coast
day-urgent messages were tossed,
forerunners of the flaring ball;

and reckoned thus: 'Let one voice fail
our sacred task, then drowns the sun;
nor could the parted chain avail
to fish him forth or in the least
appease that Rooster of the East
by whom first daylight is begun.

So, stern like destinies, we bear
the signals westward without bound;
and always heralds waiting there
will stretch and flap and pass the shout,
and still no last . . . whence—reason it out—
last is new first; the world's egg-round!

Boast across morning each to each
this toil has made our proud estate
far other than old fables teach
which call us puppets jerked for sport;
cry, every bird is in some sort
that leader clamouring at dawngate.'


## *1918-1941*

Not those patient men who knocked and were unheeded
where ignorance impeded like a flat panel swung
before the tower-stair to the dark mind of the young:
another moved beside them on the dais, at the desk—
War in a square cap, gowned and grotesque.

This was the master whose tongue did the talking:
then time became a chalking-off of dates upon the wall—
for no lad chose a calling who heard instead a call,
and just beyond a boy's years (so the lesson ran)
the one work waited fitting for a man.

None grew so tiptoe as to see the plain road, yonder,
at the hour's edge dip under to the leagues of calm before.
It was odd to break step and shamble from the door,
to plough the broad peace, and grow older, and learn pride
from the day's task met and the morrow still defied.

Distant the guns are and no wind veering
has brought them into hearing, nor yet in these lands
do they bawl between hills as between a pair of hands;
but here's what we were bred to . . . and strange it is then
to be lifting our sons up to watch the marching men.

Tattered the bewilderment I pull across my shoulders
and, shamed before beholders in this torn shirt,
like a slave to my shoes I wander unalert,
with eyes but no thought in them to mark the way I tread,
and a thought without eyes that runs lost in my head.

## The Face of the Waters

Once again the scurry of feet—those myriads
crossing the black granite; and again
laughter cruelly in pursuit; and then
the twang like a harpstring or the spring of a trap,
and the swerve on the polished surface: the soft little pads
sidling and skidding and avoiding; but soon caught up
in the hand of laughter and put back—

There is no release from the rack
of darkness for the unformed shape,
the unexisting thought
stretched half-and-half
in the shadow of beginning and that denser black
under the imminence of huge pylons—
the deeper nought;
but neither is there anything to escape,
or to laugh,
or to twang that string which is not a string but silence
plucked at the heart of silence.

Nor can there be a floor to the bottomless;
except in so far as conjecture must arrive
lungs cracking, at the depth of its dive;

where downward further is further distress
with no change in it; as if a mile and an inch
are equally squeezed into a pinch,
and retreating limits of cold mind
frozen, smoothed, defined.

Out of the tension of silence (the twanged string);
from the agony of not being (that terrible laughter
tortured by darkness); out of it all
once again the tentative migration; once again
a universe on the edge of being born:
feet running fearfully out of nothing
at the core of nothing:
colour, light, life, fearfully
becoming eyes and understanding: sound becoming ears . . .

For eternity is not space reaching
on without end to it; not time without end to it,
nor infinity working round in a circle;
but a placeless dot enclosing nothing,
the pre-time pinpoint of impossible beginning,
enclosed by nothing, not even by emptiness—
impossible: so wholly at odds with possibilities
that, always emergent and wrestling and inter-linking,
they shatter it and return to it, are all of it and part of it.
It is your hand stretched out to touch your neighbour's,
and feet running through the dark, directionless like darkness.

Worlds that were spun adrift re-enter
that intolerable centre;
indeed the widest-looping comet
never departed from it;
it alone exists.

And though, opposing it, there persists
the enormous structure of forces, laws,
as background for other coming and going,
that's but a pattern, a phase, no pause,
of ever-being-erected, ever-growing
ideas unphysically alternative
to nothing, which is the quick. You may say hills live,
or life's the imperfect aspect of a flowing
that sorts itself as hills; much as thoughts wind
selectively through mind.

The eggshell collapses
in the fist of the eternal instant;
all is what it was before.
Yet is that eternal instant
the pinpoint bursting into reality,
the possibilities and perhapses,
the feet scurrying on the floor.
It is the suspense also
with which the outward thrust
holds the inward surrender—
the stresses in the shell before it buckles under:
the struggle to magpie-morning and all life's clamour and lust;
the part breaking through the whole;
light and the clear day and so simple a goal.

## Traditional Tune

Though moonlight dapples
past time-effacement
the harbour ripples,
the candied air,

it's all deserted—
like lover from love's casement
there has departed
what found these fair.

Yet where I follow
some few hours older
and call youth shallow
from wisdom's crutch,
Life meets me, gaudy,
a rose pinned at her shoulder
for hands as greedy
as once dared touch.

O moondrowned city
be long of learning
that graver ditty
than old delight—
that song of mortals
of—over springs returning—
the flash that hurtles
through upper night.

## *Edge*

Knife's edge, moon's edge, water's edge,
graze the throat of the formed shape
that sense fills where shape vanishes:
air at the ground limit of steel,
the thin disc in the moon's curve,
land gliding out of no land.

The new image, the freed thought,
are carved from that inert bulk
where the known ends and the unknown
is cut down before it—at the mind's edge,
the knife-edge at the throat of darkness.


### *Song in Autumn*

Though we have put
white breath to its brief caper
in the early air,
and have known elsewhere
stiff fingers, frost underfoot,
sun thin as paper;


cold then was a lens
focussing sight, and showed that riggers' gear,
the spider's cables,
anchored between the immense
steel trusses of built grass. The hills were so near
you could pick up pebbles.


It is different at evening: damp rises
not crisp or definite like frost
but seeping into the blood and brain—
the end of enterprises.
And while, out of many things lost,
courage may remain,

this much is certain
from others' experience
and was indeed foretold;
noon's over; the days shorten.
Let there be no pretence;
none here likes the cold.

## Bog and Candle

### I

At the end of life paralysis or those creeping teeth,
the crab at lung or liver or the rat in the brain,
and flesh become limp rag, and sense tap of a cane—
if you would pray, brother, pray for a clean death.

for when the work you chip from age-hard earth must pause,
faced with the dark, unfinished, where day gave love and jest,
day and that earth in you shall pit you to their test
of struggle in old bog against the tug of claws.

### II

What need had such a one for light at the night's rim?
Yet in the air of evening till the medley of sound—
children and birds and traffic—settled in the profound
meditation of earth, it was the blind man's whim

to set at his wide window the warm gift of flame
and put a match to wick for sight not like his own—
for his blank eyes could pierce that darkness all have known,
the thought: 'What use the light, or to play out the game?'

Yet could disperse also the fog of that queer code
which exalts pain as evidence of some aim or end
finer than strength it tortures, so sees pain as friend—
good in itself and guiding to great ultimate good.

Then he would touch the walls of the cold place where he sat
but know the world as wider, since here, beside his hand,
this flame could reach out, out, did touch but understand . . .
Life in a man's body perhaps rayed out like that.

So it is body's business and its inborn doom
past will, past hope, past reason and all courage of heart,
still to resist among the roof-beams ripped apart
the putting-out of the candle in the blind man's room.

## This Between Us . . .

Sleep at Lovo, old chief or warrior,
once my companion days and nights together,
you in your mound, the long grass over you,
I lying above the grass beside you.
You did not chide my nearness, neither by day
my comings and goings and more impatient waiting—
stamping up and down knee-deep among weeds,
beating the damp clay into a path at your head—
nor yet by night my lesser sleep than yours
where there we lay, the two of us, under the hills,
Nasorolevu behind us, the great lonely
weight of the night—empty between the hills—
over us, and Lovo stream at our feet
rattling, bubbling, boiling as it does now
in your deaf ears and my own ears remembering.

III

Nameless forgotten chief, I came
so long after you through that gash in the range,
Tagi-na-sola (meaning the-stranger-weeps
met by this pass as enemy) that my climbing
that sideling track between bared teeth of boulders—
not fenced as once with spears but difficult still—
was to a place which enough years have changed
from just what ground you walked on who lie in it now
to surface that forgets and is other ground.
There I could reach all things that those years hoard
but found nothing your thought might share with mine
And so your blood-splash lifetime, your eating of men,
your rites and loves—were of air only, lost,
not to be entered into or understood
or lit from within. Yet there is this between us:
that your world which is gone, and my world going,
are your darkness—the passing of what was—
and mine blotting tomorrow's windowpane—
the passing of what is. Then comes the stranger.

What mast on the sea? what sail? what smoke in the sky?
Shouts from the beach! Let the young men go down.
The sun we knew sinks drowning beyond Yasawa.


J. A. R. McKELLAR

## Twelve O'Clock Boat

Only the creaking murmur of the wheel,
The trembling of the engines as they turn;
The ferry glides upon an even keel,
And Pinchgut squats in shadow hard astern . . .

The lips of ocean murmur at delay.
The lovely moon no longer will refuse,
And from the arms of darkness slips away
To tryst with young Ephesians on Vaucluse,

Naked as when some mercenary Greek
The galleys bore to Carthage stared the sky,
Feeling a wind Sicilian on his cheek,
And fell asleep with no more hope than I

Of life eternal, love, or length of days,
Dreaming he saw his Macedonian home;
Awoke, and duly went his ordered ways
To die at Zama, on the swords of Rome.

But what was moon to him, and what was sea
Two thousand years before myself was born,
Are sickle moon and silver yet to me,
Though Scipio should wait upon Cremorne.

## ETHEL ANDERSON

### Migrants

I was even wearier where I waited
In the noontide heat for the coming of night
Than the wedge-tailed swallow, the sea wayfarer,
Tired of wind and planet and the fading wave;

113

I knew no such solace as I've known them flailing
From the nick of moments in an edgeless sky,
Birds linked in the eddies of the Empyrean
To ease the spent fledgling and the failing wing;

Yet the bright Siberian snow they nest by,
The plaited rainbow of the Samarkandh lane,
Mean less to the wanderers pressing towards them
Than to me the homelight as I look backward.


PETER HOPEGOOD

## Free Martin

Here is Martin's round house;
built it is of mud.
From the lake he won it
with his hod and spud.

Came the elphin hunters
following the deer
over fell and moorland
over half a year.

Panting from the lakeside
hard before the din
comes a bonny roebuck.
Martin takes it in.

When the chase has dwindled,
Martin: says the roe;
Ask for what you will . . .
it is yours before I go.

I would like a gorget
ruddy as your coat.
I would like a white horse,
I would like a boat.

I would like a mantle
deep and dark and blue;
I would like a sharp arrow
to sever it in two.

I would like a portcullis
to set before my gate.
I would like a bonny doe
to be my bonny mate.

You shall have a gorget
ruddy as the sun;
And a horse as white as foam
and a boat, in one.

You shall have a portcullis
to set before your keep.
You shall have a silver doe
to rouse you from your sleep.

You shall have a mantle
deep and dark and blue;
you shall have a sharp arrow
to sever it in two.

Yet I charge you answer
this before I go:
Who shall wear a cloak shent
by a sharp arrow?

Martin gives for answer:
Just before the dawn
comes a naked fellow
and lays him on the lawn.

Bloody are his limbs and crown;
bloody is his track;
and cold . . . cold . . . cold
blows the wind from off the lake.

I would share my mantle
dark and blue and deep
with that bloody cold one
who troubles all my sleep;

for he may not enter here.
His place is on the lawn.
And cold . . . cold . . . cold
blows the wind about the dawn.

He should have my mantle
dark and deep and whole.
He should have its blue unshent
would it warm his soul.

But 'twould noways warm him,
not in any part,
without its sister portion
be warmed by my own heart.

His pallid breast it will not warm
into a living glow
without my own be smote in twain
by a sharp arrow.

Blood must drench our mantle
deep and dark and blue . . .
blood must stain our mantle
to a kingly hue.

His bloody limbs it may not heal
of the red wounds they bear
from the bolts of Elphin
over half a year,

until the Livid Hunter
hanging on the Oak
shall launch a levin swift to sear
in twain a seamless cloak.

Gi'n I gain our mantle
deep and dark and blue,
gi'n I gain a sharp arrow
to sever it in two,

I shall have my white horse,
I shall have my boat,
I shall have a sunrise
darting from my throat,

I shall have a portcullis
to set before my keep
and a bonny doe with coat aglow
to rouse me from my sleep.

## Dithyramb in Retrospect

I was carried to a font.
Stranger fingers marked my front.
   Significant, no doubt, the rite
   that day was day and night was night:
   yet it could not make me see.
   Lifeless was that sorcery.

Then I sought a font in Toil,
smeared my sweaty brows with Soil.
   Still by fingers strange 'twas done,
   though the fingers were my own.

Then I sought a font in Fire;
leapt I Armageddon's pyre.
   Iron set on me his hand:
   but 'twas still a stranger brand.

Then a passion smote my heart
with a devastating dart.
   Still I could in no wise see.
   Darkness ever compassed me.

With my pain I face the Sky
When my planet there must ply . . .
   And the fingers of the wind
   touch me with my Very Wand.
   Straightway know I power to see
   what the light has hid from me.

By the Wind that walks the Night
I am baptized into sight.

## MAX DUNN

### Flower of Exile

Now wanderer in hostile forests, exile
By choice among unchosen enemies,
Beneath the crooked moon he still goes seeking
On boughs of flesh the flower that never dies.
On his grey screen unfolds no daylight image,
No undistorted archetype of peace,
Except blurred letters on a broken column,
Buried where now green silences arise,
And the far-off tolling of a bell sunken
Among ships' bones and red anemones.
Yet, in a long-forgotten garden, the seed
He tossed upon a heap of stones still lies,
Its golden burden undelivered, waiting
Till he returns from barren voyages:
The lock is green with time, the key is rusted,
But through the gate sleeps his lost paradise.

### I Danced Before I Had Two Feet

I danced before I had two feet
And sang before I had a tongue;
I laughed before I had two eyes
And loved before my heart was young.

I swam before I had two hands
And held the distance in my toes
Before I heard the stars or knew
The wild compulsion of the rose.

I bore the fruit of many lives
Before I came into this day;
I knew before my grave was made
The worms eat only death away.

# BRIAN VREPONT

## *The Net-menders*

I came upon them by a strip of sea,
In a drizzle of rain mending their fishing-net,
Four swift brown hands, and lean with industry,
Shuttling the thin twine skilfully in-out, repairing the fret
Of rock-jag, shark-tooth and thresh;
He, tense as a mackerel, strong and agile,
Sea-eyed and grim as a rock, turned, and his smile
Was as the wonder of sunshine on sea-rock,
His fingers harping the net-mesh;
She on the sea-side, facing the land, took stock
Of me leisurely nearing, through half-shut eyes.
'Defence', I thought; but her mouth relaxed, went sweet
And soft as a sea-flower, her hands' enterprise
On the sea-side of the breaks in the net
Rippling the strings of the two-sided harp o' the sea,
And I thought, 'Here is where sea-melodies meet,
Mending the breakages of earth-and-sea-fret,'
And the strange great grace of simplicity came on me.

If they had angers in them, these two by the sea,
Not in the two days dwelt with them,
Watching the shuttle flying, the flat corks tied,

And the strong boat pitch-caulked for battle with the sea,
Was flaw apparent in the gem;
Their poverty, too real for pride to hide,
Gave them no envy, not even in the lamp-light
And shadows of our talk,
Not when the net was trailed and netted nought
Save weed, nor when I spoke, that unforgettable night
We fought the tide, and drifted home star-caught,
And I spoke of the hawk
Now in the dark vanished, that all day long
Circled and soared and plunged on innocence; 'Cruel life,' I
    cried;
But my cry crossed over the woman's song,
Over the zither of the boat cutting the brine, and died,
And the man said, 'It is life,'
And the boat gritted the waiting sand
With sound of a cleansing knife,
And we slept, at life's command.


## The Bomber

In a hollow of the forest
They were beyond neighbours;
He said to her, in a lift of peace
After their ecstasy—'Can it be?'
After a silence, when only the forest spoke,
He said, 'It is all roses,'
But she, more secretly listening,
Said, 'No! blue-cool cornflowers,'
But the forest, profound in nature's truth, said,
'No! It is lilies.'

There was a host about
Absorbed in secrecies,
Shut off and imprisoned in selves
Beyond good neighbourhood,
Beyond touch of friendliness,
Oneness, each separate,
Beyond dark, beyond light—
Insular insects in armour safe
Only pretending death;
Prisoned by fear.

There was no love about,
Neither in shape, sound, nor movement,
Only the protoplasm of love;
Thing ate thing, prowled and preyed,
In life foredoomed to dung;
But deaf, the man said,
'No! It is roses!'
She, with the ear of earth, said,
'It is blue-cool cornflowers.'
The forest said, 'It is
Funereal lilies!'

The lovers rose; pregnant with love,
Deaf to the moment, he cupped
A hand over her breast and they went
Home slowly in a sun
Descending over the purple hills;
The bomber roared over their dream.

# A. D. HOPE

## *Australia*

A nation of trees, drab green and desolate grey
In the field uniform of modern wars
Darkens her hills, those endless, outstretched paws
Of sphinx demolished or stone lion worn away.

They call her a young country, but they lie:
She is the last of lands, the emptiest,
A woman beyond her change of life, a breast
Still tender but within the womb is dry;

Without songs, architecture, history:
The emotions and superstitions of younger lands.
Her rivers of water drown among inland sands,
The river of her immense stupidity

Floods her monotonous tribes from Cairns to Perth.
In them at last the ultimate men arrive
Whose boast is not: 'we live' but 'we survive',
A type who will inhabit the dying earth.

And her five cities, like five teeming sores
Each drains her, a vast parasite robber-state
Where second-hand Europeans pullulate
Timidly on the edge of alien shores.

Yet there are some like me turn gladly home
From the lush jungle of modern thought, to find
The Arabian desert of the human mind,                *here is no past*
Hoping, if still from the deserts the prophets come,

123

Such savage and scarlet as no green hills dare
Springs in that waste, some spirit which escapes
The learned doubt, the chatter of cultured apes
Which is called civilization over there.

## Standardization

When, darkly brooding on this Modern Age,
The journalist with his marketable woes
Fills up once more the inevitable page
Of fatuous, flatulent, Sunday-paper prose;

Whenever the green aesthete starts to whoop
With horror at the house not made with hands
And when from vacuum cleaners and tinned soup
Another pure theosophist demands

Rebirth in other, less industrial stars,
Where huge towns thrust up in synthetic stone
And films and sleek miraculous motor-cars
And celluloid and rubber are unknown;

When, from his vegetable Sunday-school,
Emerges with the neatly maudlin phrase
Still one more Nature poet, to rant and drool
About the 'standardization of the race',

I see, stooping among her orchard trees,
The old, sound Earth, gathering her windfalls in,
Broad in the hams and stiffening at the knees,
Pause, and I see her grave, malicious grin.

For there is no manufacturer competes
With her in the mass production of shapes and things.
Over and over she gathers and repeats
The cast of a face, a million butterfly wings.

She does not tire of the pattern of a rose,
Her oldest tricks still catch us by surprise.
She cannot recall how long ago she chose
The streamlined hulls of fish, the snail's long eyes.

Love still pours into its ancient mould
The lashing seed that grows to a man again,
From whom by the same processes unfold
Unending generations of living men.

She has standardized his ultimate needs and pains;
Lost tribes in a lost language mutter in
His dreams; his science is tethered to their brains;
His guilt merely repeats Original Sin;

And beauty standing motionless before
Her mirror sees behind her, mile on mile,
A long queue in an unknown corridor,
Anonymous faces plastered with her smile.

## Soledades of the Sun and Moon

### For P. K. Page

Now the year walks among the signs of heaven,
Swinging her large hips, smiling in all her motions,
Crosses with dancing steps the Milky Valley.
Round her the primal energies rejoice;
All the twelve metaphysical creatures and the seven
Swift spheres adore her vigour; the five oceans
    Look up and hear her voice
Ring through the ebony vault, where Ara Celi
Flames, and the choiring stars at their devotions
    With pure and jubilant noise
Praise and proclaim four seasons in her belly.

Four glittering worms, they sleep curled up inside her,
The unborn children of our isolation.
Solstice or song, in swift pursuit forever
We grieve in separate festivals of light.
What winged stallion, what immortal rider
Forks those wild flanks? What milk of generation
    Fills at a thrust the bright
Throat of the womb? By what supreme endeavour
Do the chaste Muses still take inspiration
    And tune the strings aright
By the god's bow that twangs to slay and sever?

Aimer of pestilence, Lucifer of healing,
Destroyer of the piping faun, Apollo!
Join these divided hearts. In single chorus
The raving sybil and the lucid seer

Find words to the one music, each revealing
Light in the other's dark, dark in that shining, hollow
    Galactic hemisphere,
Which spins the changeless images before us.
Sign after sign, the constellations follow,
    Mirrored across the year
Where Scorpio views her house of death in Taurus.


Where the Wise Archer hangs his glittering quiver
Each son of Leda greets a heavenly brother.
As country or sex or song or birth conspire
The hemispheres set their crystal walls between.
Narcissus in air, Narcissus in the river
Drown in an alien element, or smother
    The lives towards which they lean.
Yet, through the burning circles of desire,
Immortal spirits behold, each in the other:
    His pillar of flame serene,
She, the unknown somnambulist of her fire.


Cradles of earth receive the salamander
But once at most in any generation;
Once in an age a desert tribe surprises
The solitary bird, the burning tree;
Innocent of their state, the poets wander,
Seeking the kindred of their incarnation,
    Waste land and homeless sea.
Phosphor declining as Orion rises
May for a brief hour break his isolation,
    The dying Phoenix see
New Phoenix blazing in her nest of spices.

Only in space, not time, the pattern changes:
Over your land of memory, enchanted
Glides the Celestial Swan, and in your bitter
Darkness the She-Bear shambles round the Pole;
Anvils of summer, in mine, the iron ranges
Rise from its arid heart to see the haunted
   River of Light unroll
Towards Achernar, where Hermes, the transmitter
Of spirits, herald of men and gods, has granted
   Speech between soul and soul,
And each to each the Swan and Phoenix glitter.


The mortal hearts of poets first engender
The parleying of those immortal creatures;
Then from their interchange create unending
Orbits of song and colloquies of light;
Sexes in their apocalyptic splendour
In mutual contemplation of their natures
   Transfigure or unite;
Descant and burden in diapason blending,
Urania dances, and the sacred gestures
   Become the words we write,
My lark arising or your dove descending.


For you the gods of song forgo their quarrel;
Panther and Wolf forget their former anger;
For you this ancient ceremony of greeting
Becomes a solemn apopemptic hymn.
Muses who twist the ivy with the laurel
In savage measures celebrate you, Stranger;

For you the Maenads trim
Their torches and, in order due repeating
The stately ode, invoke you. Wanderer, Ranger,
  Beyond the utmost rim
Of waters, hear the voice of these entreating!


And, as the solitary bird of passage,
Loosing her heart across the wastes of ocean,
Sees round the cliffs of home the black tide crawling,
Accept the incantation of this verse;
Read its plain words; divine the secret message
By which the dance itself reveals a notion
  That moves our universe.
In the star rising or the lost leaf falling
The life of poetry, this enchanted motion,
  Perpetually recurs.
Take, then, this homage of our craft and calling.


Put on your figures of fable: with the chalice
From which the poets alone drink wisdom, healing,
And joy that weds the thyrsus with the lyre,
Be Circe—or be my Queen of Sheba; come
Silent at nightfall to my silent palace
And read my heart, and rest; and when the wheeling
  Signs of the sky turn home,
I shall arise and show you in his byre
Among your milk-white dromedaries kneeling,
  Fierce in that lilied gloom,
My horn of gold, my unicorn of fire.


129

K

## *A Bidding Grace*

For what we are about to hear, Lord, Lord,
The dreadful judgement, the unguessed reprieve,
The brief, the battering, the jubilant chord
Of trumpets quickening this guilty dust,
Which still would hide from what it shall receive,
Lord, make us thankful to be what we must.

For what we are now about to lose, reprove,
Assuage or comfort, Lord, this greedy flesh,
Still grieving, still rebellious, still in love,
Still prodigal of treasure still unspent.
Teach the blood weaving through its intricate mesh
The sight, the solace, the silence of consent.

For what we are about to learn too late, too late
To save, though we repent with tears of blood:
The innocent ruined, the gentle taught to hate,
The love we made a means to its despair—
For all we have done or did not when we could,
Redouble on us the evil these must bear.

For what we are about to say, urge, plead,
The specious argument, the lame excuse,
Prompt our contempt. When these archangels read
Our trivial balance, lest the shabby bill
Tempt to that abjectness which begs or sues,
Leave us one noble impulse: to be still.

For what we are about to act, the lust, the lie
That works unbidden, even now restrain
This reckless heart. Though doomed indeed to die,

Grant that we may, still trembling at the bar
Of Justice in the thud of fiery rain,
Acknowledge at last the truth of what we are.

In all we are about to receive, last, last,
Lord, help us bear our part with all men born
And, after judgement given and sentence passed,
Even at this uttermost, measured in thy gaze,
Though in thy mercy, for the rest to mourn,
Though in thy wrath we stand, to stand and praise.


## The Death of the Bird

For every bird there is this last migration:
Once more the cooling year kindles her heart;
With a warm passage to the summer station
Love pricks the course in lights across the chart.

Year after year a speck on the map, divided
By a whole hemisphere, summons her to come;
Season after season, sure and safely guided,
Going away she is also coming home.

And being home, memory becomes a passion
With which she feeds her brood and straws her nest,
Aware of ghosts that haunt the heart's possession
And exiled love mourning within the breast.

The sands are green with a mirage of valleys;
The palm-tree casts a shadow not its own;
Down the long architrave of temple or palace
Blows a cool air from moorland scarps of stone.

And day by day the whisper of love grows stronger;
That delicate voice, more urgent with despair,
Custom and fear constraining her no longer,
Drives her at last on the waste leagues of air.

A vanishing speck in those inane dominions,
Single and frail, uncertain of her place,
Alone in the bright host of her companions,
Lost in the blue unfriendliness of space,

She feels it close now, the appointed season:
The invisible thread is broken as she flies;
Suddenly, without warning, without reason,
The guiding spark of instinct winks and dies.

Try as she will, the trackless world delivers
No way, the wilderness of light no sign,
The immense and complex map of hills and rivers
Mocks her small wisdom with its vast design.

And darkness rises from the eastern valleys,
And the winds buffet her with their hungry breath,
And the great earth, with neither grief nor malice,
Receives the tiny burden of her death.

## Crossing the Frontier

Crossing the frontier they were stopped in time,
Told, quite politely, they would have to wait:
Passports in order, nothing to declare,
And surely holding hands was not a crime;
Until they saw how ranged across the gate,
All their most formidable friends were there.

Wearing his conscience like a crucifix,
Her father, rampant, nursed the Family Shame;
And, armed with their old-fashioned dinner-gong,
His aunt, who even when they both were six,
Had just to glance towards a childish game
To make them feel that they were doing wrong.

And both their mothers, simply weeping floods,
Her head-mistress, his boss, the parish priest,
And the bank manager who cashed their cheques;
The man who sold him his first rubber-goods;
Dog Fido, from whose Love-life, shameless beast,
She first observed the basic facts of sex.

They looked as though they had stood there for hours;
For years; perhaps for ever. In the trees
Two furtive birds stopped courting and flew off;
While in the grass beside the road the flowers
Kept up their guilty traffic with the bees.
Nobody stirred. Nobody risked a cough.

Nobody spoke. The minutes ticked away;
The dog scratched idly. Then, as parson bent
And whispered to a guard who hurried in,
The customs-house loudspeakers with a bray
Of raucous and triumphant argument
Broke out the wedding march from *Lohengrin*.

He switched the engine off: 'We must turn back.'
She heard his voice break, though he had to shout
Against a din that made their senses reel,
And felt his hand, so tense in hers, go slack.
But suddenly she laughed and said: 'Get out!
Change seats! Be quick!' and slid behind the wheel.

And drove the car straight at them: with a harsh,
Dry crunch that showered both with scraps and chips,
Drove through them; barriers rising let them pass;
Drove through and on and on, with Dad's moustache
Beside her twitching still round waxen lips
And Mother's tears still streaming down the glass.

RONALD McCUAIG

## Betty by the Sea

Her drooping flowers dabble upon
Drooping breasts of crisp cretonne;
The thirsty sun has drained her breasts
Of milk of human interests
In babies, chatting, recipes,
Husband's pleasing lewderies
And gossip over the kitchen fence,
And left this earthy innocence;
The kindly sun has drained away
Her life, like suds on washing day,
And left her in this chair on the sands,
Clasping her flowers with laundered hands:
As though a storm of breeding-pains
And work and worry, which scoured her veins,
Had passed, she opens her tired eyes,
Like still seas, to vacant skies.

## Love Me and Never Leave Me

Love me, and never leave me,
Love, nor ever deceive me,
And I shall always bless you
If I may undress you:
   Which I heard a lover say
   To his sweetheart where they lay.

He, though he did undress her,
Did not always bless her;
She, though she would not leave him,
Often did deceive him;
   Yet they loved, and when they died
   They were buried side by side.


JAMES PICOT

## To the Rosella in the Poinsettia Tree

Beautiful bird, in as your wings as vivid
A tree, Rosella! Beautiful bird, I said:

'Your tent won't shelter you or love or me,
Red lad, these nine-o'-clocks, when Beauty looks
Pomp undue—indeed a ceremony
Too grand for the brown-eaten ribbed old livid
Wall behind of a tin factory!'

But the upward sun still burned them on
To tulip crimson from their poppy scarlet,
Those poinsettia petals, till at almost
Noon, he glowed in turn behind each moon,
Lamp, leaf,—the Wished-for-One—O, separate, crimson!—

For he seemed to burn each petal free,
Till but that Double Fire was to see—
And now there is but Light for Love to be!

## Do You Not Hear?

Do you not hear
The answer of the year? Though pale,
Full-stamened, strong, the guava blows; the young
Persimmon is so like
His leaf, you must be near
To know he is already as big in the deep
Shadow his cradle as a young love-apple.
These things were made beautiful by sleep.

## Finale

Forgive me, Lord, the callow things I say:
Thy pardon wants tomorrow as today.

We bruise the anvil for the iron-truth;
But in the morning when we go away
It is to live as though the knocks were vain;
And in the evening when we come again
It is the door we hammer for Thy ruth.

There is a jewel with Thy glory kissed
I have not fashioned in this random play.

Forgive me strangled heats and passion's mist:
Forgive me, Lord, tomorrow as today.

# IAN MUDIE

## *Underground*

Deep flows the flood,
deep under the land.
Dark is it, and blood
and eucalypt colour and scent it.
Deep flows the stream,
feeding the totem-roots,
deep through the time of dream
in Alcheringa.
Deep flows the river,
deep as our roots reach for it;
feeding us, angry and striving
against the blindness
ship-fed seas bring us
from colder waters.

## *The North-Bound Rider*

Tombstone country—
so the pioneer described it.
'Patches of tombstone country,'
he wrote, 'exist in this area; indeed
at one place the north-bound rider
observes for more than ten miles
this horrible terrain.'
The north-bound rider . . . Surely,
I thought, it must exist
for him who travels
west or east or south, besides
occurring for the eye
of him who merely northward rides.

At each of the stations round about, however,
it was always the same.
Blue would scratch his head.
'Tombstone country;
did you say tombstone country?
Never heard of it.'
And Mulga would ask:
'Who told you about it?'
And at my answer
they would give me sidelong looks.
'Books!' they would snort.
'Huh—books!'

Tombstone country . . .
Ask and ask, as I did,
I never found it.
Only, a dozen times over,
the same reply to my question:

'Tombstone country, did you say?
Never heard of it.'

. . . Yet as years pass I grow more certain
I must return to those ranges once again
and somehow reach that dreaded region
that only in my dreams I now attain
(the north-bound rider nudging at my elbow)
—ten barren miles of horrible terrain.

# REX INGAMELLS

## *Sea-chronicles*

Where old-time ships came, canvas seagull-white,
articulate around our coast, the seas
speak sailors' Spanish, Dutch and Portuguese,
mutter and roar and whisper, day and night.

Lost names are sounded, could we hear aright,
that beat the Endeavour by two centuries
inside the Barrier Reef, and mysteries
resolved for which our scholars have no light.

Voices of water tell and tell and tell
the truths we cannot guess, and sun and stars
confirm and store the facts we have not found.

The winds know how a chill foreboding fell
upon a shore, where, jostled in by spars,
lay bodies of the first invaders, drowned.

## WILLIAM HART-SMITH

### When You Touch

When you touched the cold
rail that night, you said
My touch goes home along the
steel, all the way home.

Only a road and a railway-line,
for we were between stations,
and I said, Therefore the earth,
this common earth will do.

It is the same ground, and the whole
round world round the same
air you breathe, and I, and they:
and hand on heart

is hand on every heart.

## *Drama*

Looking cautiously down they saw two men fishing,
Easing their lines above the snouts of the sharp rocks,
Advancing and retreating as the waves crashed green
And poured over their heavily-booted feet.

There was a square tank full to the brim with sea-water,
And a fire underneath where another squatted,
Tending it with sticks and sweet-smelling brushwood,
The breeze peeling a thin white vapour from the water.

And the watchers exchanged looks, and leant to look again,
Their round eyes taking in a complete drama and a complete
    picture,
Following the movements of the diminished figures,
And being hungry themselves were one body with the actors.

The tank was a new shape into their universe,
A new manipulation brought by these strangers;
And the fire beneath shot flames along its black belly.
The wind lifted a vapour from the water and silver droplets
    spun.

Fire is hot and water is cold, and water extinguishes fire;
But a sheet of iron is the secret of water brought to boiling.
The watchers, naked to the clean spring weather, come down
And merge into the picture that has only ourselves as onlookers
    now.

Curious, or deliberate theft, it does not matter:
One made to take a fish, and, plunging his arm to the elbow,
Received the full shock of the deadly West, and screamed.

## Baiamai's Never-failing Stream

Then he made of the stars, in my mind,
pebbles and clear water running over them,
linking most strangely feelings of im-
measurable remoteness with intimacy,

so that at one and the same time I
not only saw a far white mist of stars
there, far up there, but had my fingers
dabbling among those cold stones.

## Columbus Goes West

Columbus looks towards the New World,
The sea is flat and nothing breaks the rim
Of the world's disc;
He takes the sphere with him.

Day into night the same, the only change
The living variation at the core
Of this man's universe;
And silent on the silver ship he broods.

Red gouts of weed, and skimming fish, to crack
The stupefying emptiness of sea,
Night, and the unimpassioned gaze of stars . . .

And God be praised for the compass, oaths
Bawled in the fo'c'sle,
Broken heads, and wine,
Song and guitars,

The tramp of boots,
The wash and whip of brine.

## Boomerang

Behold! wood into bird and bird to wood again,
a brown-winged bird from the hand of a brown man.

Elbow of wood from flexed elbow of bone
to a swift hawk has amazingly grown

that mounts the sky, sun in its wings,
up, up, over the far tree fluttering

where it turns as if seized with doubt in the air.
Looks back down to the man carved there

and, afraid of the gift of sudden blood,
beats back to his heart and melts once more to wood.

ROLAND ROBINSON

## Casuarina

The last, the long-haired casuarina
stands upon the hillside where,
against the turquoise night of those first
yellow stars, she shakes her hair.

She shakes her hair out in her singing
of cliffs and caves and waterfalls,
and tribes who left the lichened sandstone
carved in gods and animals.

This is her country: honeyeaters
cry out its aboriginal name
where on her ridges still the spear-tall
lilies burn in flame and flame.

I listen, and our legend says not
more than this dark singing tree,
although her golden flowering lover
lies slain beside the winter sea.

## I Breathed into the Ash

I breathed into the ash,
I called upon the fire:
The hidden sleeping flower,
To waken and aspire.

I fed, with sheltering hand,
brush of the dead tea-tree
as incense rose between
the gums above the sea.

I breathe upon and bare
at flesh's, fibre's cost,
the spirit's coal unless
it darken and be lost,

be lost and never raise
its frankincense uncurled,
its clear flame from the ash,
the ruin of the world.

## The Rock-lily's Pale Spray

The rock-lily's pale spray,
like sunlight, halts my way
up through the unpierced hush
of birdless blue-grey bush.
The rocks crouch on their knees
in earth, torsos of trees
and limb-boughs lead up where
the cliff-face scales the air.
Out from you, rock, my friend,
I lean and, reaching, bend
the scentless pale spray back
to me and see the black
spots in each orchid-flower.
O, my love, what power
keeps you curled and bound?

Tormented, the earth's round
begins again. What rock
holds you where you lock
yourself from me? Alone
this spray breaks from the stone.

## The Desert (6)

Travelling again, his swag
tossed in the rack above his head,
he thought about his mates: 'You'll find
gibbers and bloody sand,' they'd said.

He watched the desert wheeling round.
A symbol of his mind's despair,
alone out on the plain a yellow
whirlwind writhed through trembling air.

He closed his eyes against the scene.
Then, jolted, jerked awake again—
red sandridges beneath a merciless
sky shut in the halted train.

And there, unloading sleepers, men,
the fettlers, with gaunt faces spoiled
by lusts, by exile, trod the desert
parakelia as they toiled.

His mental hell looked out upon
this other hell at last made known.          /
He wiped his sweating face and in each
ravaged face he found his own.

Ahead, the locomotive's scream
called on its freight of heavy cars.
The train ran on, beneath a turquoise
night, the galaxies of stars.

When daylight, delicate, parrot-breasted,
dissolved the stars, the moon's white rind,
scenting the wind, he knew that heaven
or hell were regions of the mind.

## ELIZABETH RIDDELL

### News of a Baby

Welcome, baby, to the world of swords
And deadlier words.
We offer you a rough bed, and tears at morning,
And soon a playground
Bounded by ice and stones,
A buttonhole of thorns,
A kiss on war's corner.

We promise you, baby,
The stumble of fear in the heart,
The lurch of fear in the bones.

Painted upon your mother's cheek already
I see the dark effusion of your blood,
Bending already beside her patient chair the bandaged ghosts.

Welcome, baby, no dread thing will be omitted.
We are your eager hosts.


## Country Tune

As I went out to walk
Beside the river flowing
I saw what I'd not hoped to see:
A black man washing a white horse.
That's how the world was going.

He washed the horse's tail
And plaited it with yellow.
The wild-west show had come to town.
That's how I saw the high white horse
And the brave black fellow.

The wild hawks flew above the smoke,
Above the river flowing;
The drunken cowboy stumbled past
And his long legs without his will
Took him where he was going.

I saw his eyes of bitter blue,
Who crossed my path unknowing,
Who would leap over my head that night
Over the tentpole, over the stars,
Over the river flowing.

I never hope to see again
The white horse decked in yellow,
The horse, the hawks, the river in flood,
The cowboy's eyes of bitter blue
Or the brave black fellow.

## Forebears

### I. *The Map*

O search the heart and belly you may find
The map of blood and it may have some meaning
But as for me as spring burns into summer and the blind
Suns follow each other to indifferent dark
I will embrace my other cousin, death,
Who long ago lay with my ancestors.

### II. *The Reverend Edward Smith*

By Waggon Hill he went
Forgiving his parish,
His left and right neighbours,
His wife in her narrow bed
The sheets to her chin,
The keeper of the inn,
The cold man in the watch-house
His cook and acquaintance,
Squire Rat in his high boots
And Lord and Lady Mouse.

But they not so lavish
With tender excuses
Refused to condone

His meagre black legs,
His long cold fingers,
The sighing of his prayers
On light bright mornings,
His hauntings and warnings.
And now he is dead
They avoid the stone
And the thin rim of grass
On his pious bone.

### III. *John Teague*

He twined the country like a briar in the fair weather
But when the autumn gales
Tore at the stubborn roots of rocks and trees
Who lit his lamp?
For other men left home to live like saints or die like dogs
But he to practise divination.

The old women would pay him a penny to twitch
The bowels with fear
(Somewhat better than a witch
Because at least a man)
But the farmer would not hear
Ill omen of the harvest till it failed
And then they set the louts, the priests and fire,
The girls crying, and horses and men, the bishop in red
With hounds and prayer to run and read him out.

The village shuddered back into its dust
And he with blood about his head
Threaded the country like a briar,
But when the gales of autumn shook the world
Who lit his lamp?

He could endure the rods across his back
But not the woman and child beside the hearth.
He was John Teague
Who left his cobbler's shop
To practise divination.

IV. *Montfort Lee and Peter Cockerill*

When the ships *Nimbus* and *Pacific Fortune*
Slid under the southing star
To Hobart Town came I in the blood of Montfort Lee
And Peter Cockerill
(Of Bankbourne in this parish, deeply mourned)
Came I in their round pale eyes and pale smooth hair
And with them planted quinces, pears and wheat,
And with them rose at dawn to be a farmer,
And with them drank
(Gentry's white cuffs below the jacket sleeves)
Cider at Norfolk.
I was the seed they sowed when nothing stirred
Across the river but a kingfisher
Abreast of morning.
(Who laid the hopfields wide and planted vines,
And built a house of stone, and sailed a boat,
And went to marriages and funerals,
And matched each other's daughters with their sons,
And rode their horses by the willow-trees,
And seldom read a book or sang a song.)

V. *Mary Lomax*

Here is the woman with the face of pearl and rose,
The great madonna of misunderstanding, she
With laces at her wrist and the unearthly glow
Of ritual in her evening's arbour pose.

My mother's mother's mother, she in paint
And gilt by secondary artists set
Upon the wall. And all her axioms lie
As shattered mirrors round her, and the faint
Tinkle of teacups dies, and dies away.
Nothing is left of all she had to say.

VI. *The Man from Richmond*

The man from Richmond ran before
The lads upon his stumbling heel
Past the church and past the store,
Past the smith and the millwheel,
Past the rhododendrons drowned
Pale, pale, under the rain,
Ran, ran until he found
Shelter where the hawthorned lane
Turned to the meadow. There he lay,
Put his cheek to the earth and wept,
And cries of idiot died away,
And the man slept.
He the father, he the fool,
Caught between the hill and stream,
Between the cliff and the shallow pool,
The people and the dream.
He the zany, he the clod
Lying under the hawthorn-tree
Wept because he was not God.
He was I and I am he.

## JOHN QUINN

## *A Foxhole for the Night*

'*Now I lay me down to sleep . . .*'

Once if a man were dead and given to the earth
At least he'd sleep dry;
At least a coffin keeps the water out.

But this is a grave designed for the living,
Skilfully fashioned in the hot, red earth
And heaped with clotted soil about its edges.

Here, in his groundsheet shroud, a man can lie
Muffled in darkness, like a cocoon-swathed grub,
Until the rain-washed dawn
Comes with its weary bone-sore resurrection.

But the dawn is an unreality
Beyond an eternity of minutes.

The clumsy night is fidgeting with sound;
The running feet of the rain on the leaves,
The tired creaking of a dying tree,
The edged, violin whine of mosquitoes.

And water reaches down these walls of earth
And twists warm, flowing fingers
Indecently through sodden clothes.

The consciousness of earth
And an unwashed body
Is a sick taste in the mouth
And a thickness in the throat.

153

And time can end with a movement in the vines.
A grenade's iron voice will tell of the ending
Or the tongue of a knife will whisper it.

*'Gentle Jesus, meek and mild,*
*Look upon a little child.'*

## DOUGLAS STEWART

### *Old Iron*

There are no instructions here for that dazzling man,
So frail in front of the engine, who one fine day
Will leap to the track and switch the points, they say,
And save the time from disaster, set the great wheels
Roaring at last on the true, the only way;

No more than a lump of iron for that man to look at
As I am looking while the crabs scuttle and hide
And the backs of the limpets dry as the seaweed has dried
To the stillness of stone, and the wrack cast up by the sea
Rusts in the sun and awaits the returning tide.

One of those weathered and very mad old men
Who live alone in their humpies, outlaws alike
From the holiday crowds who snatch at the waves and shriek
Like gulls at a meatworks, and whatever goal or disaster
Or mere receding distance our time will strike,

One of those withered and very mad old men
Concerned with their own slow rusting in natural leisure
Should be here with me, is here in my mind to treasure
This twisted bit of a ship, this battered junk,
And stretch his hand to the iron with a cry of pleasure,

Though nobody else, unless some wandering boy,
Is likely to spare it a glance. If a dumb yearning
Calls iron, after the hammering and the burning,
Back to its native earth, this has its wish:
Seabird and fish accept it as rock returning,

And as flesh and bone of the earth it takes the sun
And glows with life, or receives the sea and crumbles.
And now as always when the mind's old madman stumbles
On some such rock, and pauses, and fills with light
At an apparition of Earth, his hand trembles

And stretches out to the simple touch of the iron
As towards another hand, or to warm spring air,
Water or tree or stone, in a gesture of prayer
And sweet communion with things that accept in peace
The rhythms of earth beyond our control or care.

Lava on Egmont, shellrock at Mangamingi,
There were always sacred rocks and sacred trees,
And beside the breakwater cutting the violent seas
At far New Plymouth like a searchlight thrust in a storm,
A gigantic rusty anchor took its ease;

And far away back into childhood at Opunake
Was a shaft of iron in a rock, so deeply thrust
No giant could shake it though spray had flaked it with rust;
And no one could tell us why it was driven there
By the old mysterious men, themselves now dust.

What shall we say, old madman, of this old iron,
Meteorite on a lonely Australian reef
From the age's whirling planet of hope and grief?
Iron that stands like the earth's accusing ghost
In city buildings, iron that without relief

Roars on the rails of the world, both track and engine
For the whole adventure and drive of the urgent mind,
Lies calmly here, forgetting tormented mankind
In the older life of the earth where the simple creatures
Obey their natures and the rock is dumb and blind.

And likely enough, one of those mad old men
Will creep from his hole when the age has crashed at last
And stare at the wreck of iron and mutter aghast
'So the blind rush came to this; the earth has got them.'
But the old man hides in a hole; we thunder past,

Committed to high adventure, and what we have seen
Who cannot see our far-off stopping place,
Of the life of the earth glowing or crumbling in grace,
Is half a meeting in joy and half a goodbye,
Like seeing in the rain at night a woman's face.

## Terra Australis

Captain Quiros and Mr William Lane,
Sailing some highway shunned by trading traffic
Where in the world's skull like a moonlit brain
Flashing and crinkling rolls the vast Pacific,

Approached each other zigzag, in confusion,
Lane from the west, the Spaniard from the east,
Their flickering canvas breaking the horizon
That shuts the dead off in a wall of mist.

'Three hundred years since I set out from Lima
And off Espiritu Santo lay down and wept
Because no faith in men, no truth in islands,
And still unfound the shining continent slept;

'And swore upon the Cross to come again
Though fever, thirst and mutiny stalked the seas
And poison spiders spun their webs in Spain,
And did return, and sailed three centuries,

'Staring to see the golden headlands wade
And saw no sun, no land, but this wide circle
Where moonlight clots the waves with coils of weed
And hangs like silver moss on sail and tackle,

'Until I thought to trudge till time was done
With all except my purpose run to waste;
And now upon this ocean of the moon,
A shape, a shade, a ship, and from the west!'

## II

'What ship?' 'The Royal Tar!' 'And whither bent?'
'I seek the new Australia.' 'I, too, stranger;
Terra Australis, the great continent
That I have sought three centuries and longer;

'And westward still it lies, God knows how far,
Like a great golden cloud, unknown, untouched,
Where men shall walk at last like spirits of fire
No more by oppression chained, by sin besmirched.'

'Westward there lies a desert where the crow
Feeds upon poor men's hearts and picks their eyes;
Eastward we flee from all that wrath and woe
And Paraguay shall yet be Paradise.'

'Eastward,' said Quiros, as San Pedro rolled,
High-pooped and round in the belly like a barrel,
'Men tear each other's entrails out for gold;
And even here I find that men will quarrel.'

'If you are Captain Quiros you are dead.'
'The report has reached me; so is William Lane.'
The dark ships rocked together in the weed
And Quiros stroked the beard upon his chin:

'We two have run this ocean through a sieve
And though our death is scarce to be believed
Seagulls and flying-fish were all it gave
And it may be we both have been deceived.'

### III

'Alas, alas, I do remember now;
In Paradise I built a house of mud
And there were fools who could not milk a cow
And idle men who would not though they could.

'There were two hundred brothers sailed this ocean
To build a New Australia in the east
And trifles of money caused the first commotion
And one small cask of liquor caused the last.

'Some had strange insects bite them, some had lust,
For wifeless men will turn to native women,
Yet who could think a world would fall in dust
And old age dream of smoke and blood and cannon

'Because three men got drunk?' 'With Indian blood
And Spanish hate that jungle reeked to Heaven;
And yet I too came once, or thought I did,
To Terra Australis, my dear western haven,

'And broke my gallows up in scorn of violence,
Gave land and honours, each man had his wish,
Flew saints upon the rigging, played the clarions:
Yet many there were poisoned by a fish

'And more by doubt, and so deserted Torres
And sailed, my seamen's prisoner, back to Spain.'
There was a certain likeness in the stories
And Captain Quiros stared at William Lane.

## IV

Then, 'Hoist the mainsail!' both the voyagers cried,
Recoiling each from each as from the devil;
'How do we know that we are truly dead
Or that the tales we tell may not be fable?

'Surely I only dreamed that one small bottle
Could blow up New Australia like a bomb?
A mutinous pilot I forbore to throttle
From Terra Australis send me demented home?

'The devil throws me up this Captain Quiros,
This William Lane, a phantom not yet born,
This Captain Quiros dead three hundred years,
To tempt me to disaster for his scorn—

'As if a blast of bony breath could wither
The trees and fountains shining in my mind,
Some traveller's tale, puffed out in moonlit weather,
Divert me from the land that I must find!

'Somewhere on earth that land of love and faith
In Labor's hands—the Virgin's—must exist,
And cannot lie behind, for there is death,
So where but in the west—but in the east?'

At that the sea of light began to dance
And plunged in sparkling brine each giddy brain;
The wind from Heaven blew both ways at once
And west went Captain Quiros, east went Lane.

## *The Sunflowers*

'Bring me a long sharp knife for we are in danger;
I see a tall man standing in the foggy corn
And his high, shadowy companions.'—'But that is no stranger,
That is your company of sunflowers; and at night they turn
Their dark heads crowned with gold to the earth and the dew
So that indeed at daybreak, shrouded and silent,
Filled with a quietness such as we never knew,
They look like invaders down from another planet.
And now at the touch of light from the sun they love'—
'Give me the knife. They move.'

## *Helmet Orchid*

Oh such a tiny colony
Set amongst all eternity
Where the great bloodwoods stand!
It is the helmet orchid
That will not lift itself
Higher than a fallen leaf
But waits intent and secret
Leaning its ear to the ground.

What could it hear but silence?
Yet where the orchid listens
Low in its purple hood
Among the trees' immensity,
Out of the depth of the world
Dark and rainy and wild
Sounding through all eternity
Silence like music flowed.

## *The Silkworms*

All their lives in a box! What generations,
What centuries of masters, not meaning to be cruel
But needing their labour, taught these creatures such patience
That now though sunlight strikes on the eye's dark jewel
Or moonlight breathes on the wing they do not stir
But like the ghosts of moths crouch silent there.

Look, it's a child's toy! There is no lid even,
They can climb, they can fly, and the whole world's their tree;
But hush, they say in themselves, we are in prison.
There is no word to tell them that they are free,
And they are not; ancestral voices bind them
In dream too deep for wind or word to find them.

Even in the young, each like a little dragon
Ramping and green upon his mulberry leaf,
So full of life, it seems, the voice has spoken:
They hide where there is food, where they are safe,
And the voice whispers, 'Spin the cocoon,
Sleep, sleep, you shall be wrapped in me soon.'

Now is their hour, when they wake from that long swoon;
Their pale curved wings are marked in a pattern of leaves,
Shadowy for trees, white for the dance of the moon;
And when on summer nights the buddleia gives
Its nectar like lilac wine for insects mating
They drink its fragrance and shiver, impatient with waiting.

M

They stir, they think they will go. Then they remember
It was forbidden, forbidden, ever to go out;
The Hands are on guard outside like claps of thunder,
The ancestral voice says Don't, and they do not.
Still the night calls them to unimaginable bliss
But there is terror around them, the vast, the abyss.

And here is the tribe that they know, in their known place,
They are gentle and kind together, they are safe for ever,
And all shall be answered at last when they embrace.
White moth moves closer to moth, lover to lover.
There is that pang of joy on the edge of dying—
Their soft wings whirr, they dream that they are flying.

## EVE LANGLEY

### *Native-born*

In a white gully among fungus red
   Where serpent logs lay hissing at the air,
I found a kangaroo. Tall, dewy, dead,
   So like a woman, she lay silent there.
Her ivory hands, black-nailed, crossed on her breast,
   Her skin of sun and moon hues, fallen cold.
Her brown eyes lay like rivers come to rest
   And death had made her black mouth harsh and old.
Beside her in the ashes I sat deep
   And mourned for her, but had no native song
To flatter death, while down the ploughlands steep
   Dark young Camelli whistled loud and long,
'Love, liberty, and Italy are all.'
   Broad golden was his breast against the sun.

I saw his wattle whip rise high and fall
   Across the slim mare's flanks, and one by one
She drew the furrows after her as he
   Flapped like a gull behind her, climbing high,
Chanting his oaths and lashing soundingly,
   While from the mare came once a blowing sigh.
The dew upon the kangaroo's white side
   Had melted. Time was whirling high around,
Like the thin wommera, and from heaven wide
   He, the bull-roarer, made continuous sound.
Incarnate lay my country by my hand:
   Her long hot days, bushfires, and speaking rains,
Her mornings of opal and the copper band
   Of smoke around the sunlight on the plains.
Globed in fire-bodies the meat-ants ran
   To taste her flesh and linked us as we lay,
For ever Australian, listening to a man
   From careless Italy, swearing at our day.
When, golden-lipped, the eagle-hawks came down
   Hissing and whistling to eat of lovely her,
And the blowflies with their shields of purple brown
   Plied hatching to and fro across her fur,
I burnt her with the logs, and stood all day
   Among the ashes, pressing home the flame
Till woman, logs, and dreams were scorched away,
   And native with night, that land from whence they came.

## *Australia*

The brown round of the continent tonight
Rises up, shoulder on shoulder, searching for the sun;
And all the white French rains that once took flight
Into the earth, rise slowly, one by one,
Remembering Villon who left a rag on every tree.
Perhaps he walked Australia long ago,
Mourning for all those women white and sad as snow.
Verlaine perhaps enchanted by our seas
Cried in his lyric voice that purple hours
Lay waxen-mitred in our purple flowers . . .
The wildflowers of Australia; a thin brown
Veil of lost Autumn is somehow caught around
Their stalks unspeaking, as though Springtime at the core
Was a small child lost in the bush for ever more.

KENNETH MACKENZIE

## *Confession*

All I have got of wealth and wisdom, I
    have spent too hungrily on wine and men,
fearing that some tomorrow I should die
    rich, wise and loveless, into dust again,
my laughter never loosed, my tears unshed,
    cold, virtuous corpse stretched on a feather bed.

This spendthrift hunger, whetted on this fear,
   bullied its bread, ate like a famished beast
in watchful rage, and never did forbear,
   but snatched at every platter of the feast—
love, hatred, friendship, charity,
   malice and kindness—all were one to me.


I lived full selfishly while time allowed,
   cast conscience out, invited in despair,
lay down with joy, walked lonely with the crowd,
   read, wrote and ravished all I thought was fair,
kept much, and lost the much I could not keep,
and found, like others, life's best bliss was sleep.


So now, sprawled dead upon the plain of Time,
   churned by the worms of living memories,
I see I have been wise to feel no crime
   in spending all on these eternities
of men and wine, to buy on earth a heaven
Such as to better men was never given.


## Caesura

Sometimes at night when the heart stumbles and stops
a full second endless the endless steps
that lead me on through this time terrain
without edges and beautiful terrible
are gone never to proceed again.

Here is a moment of enormous trouble
when the kaleidoscope sets unalterable
and at once without meaning without motion
like a stalled aeroplane in the middle sky
ready to fall down into a waiting ocean.

Blackness rises. Am I now to die
and feel the steps no more and not see day
break out its answering smile of hail all's well
from east full round to east and hear the bird
whistle all creatures that on earth do dwell?

Not now. Old heart has stopped to think of a word
as someone in a dream by far too weird
to be unlikely feels a kiss and stops
to praise all heaven stumbling in all his senses . . .
and suddenly hears again the endless steps.


## The Snake

Withdrawing from the amorous grasses
from the warm and luscious water
the snake is soul untouched by both
nor does the fire of day through which it passes
mark it or cling. Immaculate navigator
it carries death within its mouth.

Soul is the snake that moves at will
through all the nets of circumstance
like the wind that nothing stops,

immortal movement in a world held still
by rigid anchors of intent or chance
and ropes of fear and stays of hopes.

It is the source of all dispassion
the voiceless life above communion
secret as the spring of wind
nor does it know the shames of self-confession
the weakness that enjoys love's coarse dominion
or the betrayals of the mind.

Soul is the snake the cool viator
sprung from a shadow on the grass
quick and intractable as breath
gone as it came like the everlasting water
reflecting God in immeasurable space—
and in its mouth it carries death.

## Legerdemain

Ah me the hand upon the body
   the whorled speech
that sings from fingertips a wordless melody
   mounting with the delicate increasing touch
   to a long cry in the mind can never reach
   the end of the search.

Night has a thousand I O U's
   signed with sighs
shaken out of the blood that floods imperious
   the flesh touched delicately and by day these
   flutter unhonoured along habitual byways
   past averted eyes.

Or perhaps one that said *tomorrow*
　　is redeemed
by accident on the stair or in the mirror
　　where eyes look curiously into eyes doomed
　　for ever to look back curiously or dimmed
　　by what they dreamed.


For not eyes but hands only can see
　　in night's alley
that leads from nowhere and keeps busy
　　the shuddering direction-finder love's ally
　　pointing a staggering track to melancholy
　　through heaven's valley.


Ah me the seeing skin reports
　　certain replies
signalling a hasty offering of transports
　　and through the dark viaduct the eyeless music plays
　　with drums diminishing and frantic pleas
　　*keep moving please.*


The hand upon the body dies instead
　　of reason dying
though for some moments consciousness insisted
　　reason had died in the divine undoing
　　of ties with earth.
　　　　　　　Sense now steadying
hears spirit crying.

## JOHN BLIGHT

*Becalmed*

Above and below the ship, this blue:
No cloud, no island, and which of two
Suns was celestial, submarine?
Each sailor shrugged. Who'd ever been
South of the Line . . . who knew . . . who knew?

There was a vessel in the sky—
Towering above, or below the eye?
If only something would drift past,
Seaweed or cloud to foul its mast.
Why should it, too, becalmed thus, lie?

Below and above, the seeming sea
Like a great eye which dreamily
Sees nothing, and by nothing is seen;
A waking that may, may not, have been.
'Which of us now is you, is me?'

Everything double under the sun;
And doubly doubled to prove which one
Is under which, which sun above.
'God, if the counterpart would move.'
But the movement there or here is none.

'Silver's a man is full of cunning;
Monkey, he is on the taffrail running;
Agile, he props and dives right in.
One rises to meet him with a grin.
Head strikes head with a smack that's stunning.

169

'No more Silver, he's under the sea;
Or up in the sky, or where is he?'
Lost in the ether, south of the Line;
The eight bells rang, but we heard nine:
And where are we, and where are we?

Lord, it is dark. The two suns met
In a blaze of flame we won't forget:
And which ate which, we could not say;
But night came on and at close of day
We cheered. 'All's not proved double yet.'

Too soon, too soon! The moon that rose
Split into two, like silver shoes:
One walked the sky, one walked the sea;
But which walked which was strange to me:
For south of the Line, who knows . . . who knows?

'This is the other half,' I said.
'Since Egypt, here they've buried the dead,
Under the earth and south of the Line.'
The eight bells rang and we heard nine.
'We are they whom the mermaids wed.'

Doomed on a ship that is dead, becalmed;
In a winding sheet of blue, embalmed.
'Friend, it is doubly strange I feel,
No-one will credit our plight was real;
We dead, in a ship that is dead, becalmed.'

## *The Cat-o'-nine-tails*

Given the 'Cat', it was not only that he ran
A gauntlet of whips—one could bear that
Before the mast in a salt gale—but a man
Could not rally at those words, 'Convict rat'.

The delirious Cat striking with its nine
Tails, vigour and abandon of nine lives,
Mauling him, 'Convict rat'. How refine
Punishment with humour better with knives?

Cheap gibe, the Cat. It sprang again, again;
And pain filled in the hollows between ribs.
'Give him the Cat,' said voices in his brain;
'Convict rat . . . we'll break his blasted nibs.'

'Cat . . . Cat . . . give him the Cat.' He remembered
Sentence and pretence of humour grim:
And, when he felt through torture one dismembered,
Down from the triangle they bundled him.

What niceties of morning between bars
Matched his red scars; what sun's salve
Mended his hide? Better if scimitars
Descend now to quarter or halve

His striped agony—striped like a cat.
That humour would intrude. He rallied now . . . .
Milady's kitten? How he grinned at that,
Grimaces that would make one wonder how

Solace was in this as the kitten came—
'It would have done this deed; remember that,
Convict rat. It would have done the same!'
He fondled with steeled heart Milady's cat.

## Crab

Shellfish and octopus, and all the insane
Thinking of the undersea, to us is lost.
At most is food, in our higher plane.
But, what of this submarine ghost—
Life, without its meddling monkey? Can
The crab regenerate into prototype merman?
Sea, of nightmare pressure and mask—
Green faces in the gloom—what is your task
In creation; or is it over? Has space
Such aquariums of planets trapped? Was
Eden thus? Oh, pressures which the lace
Sponge of the brain survives. What has
The life of the sea of my ignorance,
But such creatures; much of this wild-shaped chance!

## Stonefish and Starfish

These are the first shapes: stonefish and starfish.
Imagine the stone falling, tumbling down the scree
Through the upper atmosphere. Here you may wish
To see a stone move, too; but the cobbles under the sea
Stare patently—dead pupils. Oh, roll a cobble
To life, even such lowly life, till it swims like a bubble . . .
I looked longing, too, into the lonely deeps
But knew I watched ages after the first star.
If I could will life there, raise it by steps
To perfection, it would be as we are.
Starfish, I know you, now, staring as I have
Where a star would long gaze for its image to move . . .
These are the first shapes, life in its first steps.
See, now, man gazes into the outer deeps.

## Sea-Level

Over this flat-pan sea, this mud haven,
this shelf of the sea-floor, sea-birds paddle
and the red mud raddles the sea.
You are on creation's level. Proven
your lowly origin, where, in one puddle,
sea-snails and your toes agree—
the same spasms and rhythms. Stub
on a rock, or a sharp stab of a beak;
they draw in. Pain is the one language
spoken to them. You, in the sky, snub
your feet. Impediments! But can you take
your brain's cloud and drift, disengage
those 'body's worms'? Try: disconnect
the thought from their feeling, and soon the soul is wrecked.

## A Cup of Sea-water

I had no thought for a poem, so I wrote
casually of the sea. The sea is
a common subject, and easily
described—for who doesn't know of a boat
and sand and rocks and what the sea is?
I wrote of the sea, and I spoke of it breezily;
but not in a poem—for who doesn't know
that a poem couldn't capture the sea,
save as a cup holds it? Then the sea tastes
warm and not unlike blood; and though
it has water's colourless anonymity,
like blood it is all too savage to drink, and wastes
and is thrown away, once you taste its fierce flavour
which is all I will you to taste, my few words to savour.


HAROLD STEWART

## Dialogue of the Way
### (For C. T. Brown)

*Wu Tao-tzŭ*, the greatest of Chinese painters.
*Hui Nêng*, the Sixth Patriarch of Ch'an Buddhism.

Earliest spring, and clouds at dawn are few.
The rising sky is sharp and chilly blue,
Clear as a sapphire, where an upward glow
Lights the eastern horizon from below.
Like prunus-blossom floating on the floes
Of cracking river-ice, the clouds dispose
Petals thereon, incomparably white,
Which dawn has filled with crisp, silver light.

Now bubbles grain the ice, and frigid rivers
Shake their backs and fracture into shivers.
Now the watered ice-sheet rapidly breaks
Up into jagged and congested cakes.
Streams are released and eastward start to flow,
A frozen slush, at first, with mud and snow;
Till free their sparkling sapphire waters gush
And heave their jostling splinters in their rush
A crystal wreckage high along the shore.
The last wild storm of winter stripped and tore
Clouds of white prunus-blossom: here they strew
The ice, a crackled field of deeper blue.


And while the China sky receives a glaze
Of azure, on this first of fresh spring days,
The painter and the patriarch prepare
To set out from the mountain temple, where
They have found lodging all the winter through.
Wu is amused but puzzled, as they do,
By Hui Nêng, whose composite attire
Prompts his curiosity to enquire:


*Wu Tao-tzǔ*

'Now, Master Hui Nêng, what are you at?
I see you have assumed the formal hat
Of an orthodox Confucian; yet you wear
The robe of Buddha's followers, and bear
A staff for pilgrimage; you even use,
To end this odd assortment, Taoist shoes!
Why are you dressed in all of these together?'

175

### Hui Nêng

'The hat protects my head in rainy weather;
The robe gives warmth against a freezing day;
The staff and shoes support me on my way.
And mind you now, I mean but what I say:
I don't indulge in myth or metaphor!'

### Wu Tao-tzŭ

'I am no wiser than I was before.
But since you are enlightened, tell me, sir:
When from the Eightfold Path my footsteps err,
How shall I follow it with faltering tread?'

### Hui Nêng

'Oh, just keep on walking straight ahead.'

But Wu is troubled as to what is meant,
And silent, as they start on their descent.
Already on the slopes the snow had thinned
When, last night, a rough but humid wind
Blew up the fog, blew up the tepid rain
That melt the snowbanks down to earth again;
And honeycomb the smoothly moulded shapes
And domes of snow, which trickles and escapes.
The mounds of glass in liquefaction wane,
As warmer waters in the flooded lakes
Dissolve away the final icy flakes:
Signs that the thaw's revolt has overthrown
The dynasty of frost, to found its own.

### Wu Tao-tzŭ

'You tell me that you use no sleight of speech,
And yet your words are wild; they do not teach
But tease me with a meaning out of reach.
Enough of these evasions. Show me now
In what direction I must follow Tao.'

### Hui Nêng

'The hills and valleys at this time of year
When winter thaws, and spring is almost freed,
Invite you to explore them. There are here
No crossroads and no by-ways to mislead;
Nor are there walls or ditches that might baulk
Your legs from taking some delightful walk.
You need no map or guide to find your way.
Follow your nose: you cannot go astray,
No matter what direction, east or west.'

### Wu Tao-tzŭ

'You mean to put my patience to the test;
But I will make you yield your secret yet.
Where lies the Middle Way?'

### Hui Nêng

                          'Your feet are set
Upon it here and now. Before your eyes
The pathway trodden by the Buddha lies.
Does language still obscure it from your sight?
Put your left foot forward, then your right!'

Exasperated by the monk's absurd
Instruction, Wu proceeds without a word.

N

The ridges have grown balder overnight,
With isles of russet in their seas of white.
The land is left as chequered as the bark
Of bare white-poplars, where it splits to mark
Their silver limbs with diamonds of dark.
And half-exposed recline the lower hills,
Lyrical with a choir of little rills
That seek the sea with music through the plains,
Carrying off the winter in their veins;
Whose silver tributaries lace the land
Like veins branching in a poplar's hand.
The day approaching now with radiant beam,
Vapours exhale, and all the valleys steam.
Here is a world in deliquescence, where
Tongues of evaporation lick the air;
And on all sides is heard the sinking sound,
Faint but distinct, uttered by drinking ground.


## J. P. McAULEY

### *The Blue Horses*
(In honour of Franz Marc)

#### I

What loud wave-motioned hooves awaken
Our dream-fast members from the cramp of sleep?
The tribal images are shaken
And crash upon their guardians. The skies
Are shivered like a pane of glass.

Progeny of winds, sea-forms, earth-bestriders
From the blue quarries of their natal hills

Terribly emerging to their riders,
Blue Horses lift their neighing trumpets to the moon!
They stamp among the spiritual mills
That weave a universe from our decay:
The specious outline crumbles at the shock
Of visionary hooves, and in dismay
Men hide among the tumbled images.

The silver trumpets strike the moon!
O grasp the mane with virgin hand:
Beneath the knocking of the magic hoof
New spaces open and expand.
For in the world are spaces infinite
And each point is a mighty room
Where flowers with strange faces bloom
In the amazing light;
And every little crystal minute
Has many aeons locked within it
Within whose crystal depths we see
Times upon times eternally.

## II

The whittled moon
Lies on the steep incline of night
Flanked by a stair of fading stars.
The hooves are silent.
Chimney-stacks
Pour their first smoke-trail across
The lightening cloud-bars.
The first wheel clacks
On grinding gears,
The pulley whirrs upon its boss.

Naked you lie and your own silence keep,
The arms of love are laid aside in sleep.
Soon it will be day like other days:
I cannot hold this hour in my hand
Nor press
Its image on a substance beyond time.
Possess!
But we are never in possession
And nothing stays at our command.
Possess!
Yet day comes on.
The delicate steel cranes manoeuvre
Like giant birds above their load;
The high song of the tyres is heard
Along the whitening road.
Possess!
All things escape us, as we too escape.
We have owned nothing and have no address
Save in the poor constriction
Of a legal or poetic fiction.
He that possesses is possessed
And falsifies perception lest
The visionary hooves break through
The simple seeming world he knew.
Possess!
His wife hangs lace across the view
And all they know of lucid lithe Septembers
Is guilty dreams and itching members.


The harbour derricks swing their load upon the shore.
The sacred turbines hum, the factories
Set up their hallowed roar.

Men must awake betimes and work betimes
To furnish the supplies of war.
For some shall work and some possess
And all shall read the morning papers
And from the world's ripped entrails there displayed
Haruspicate the trends of love and trade.

Sleep no more, for while you sleep
Our love is stolen by the cheating sun
And angry frightened men destroy
Our peace with diktat, pact, and gun.
The old men of the tribe go mad
And guard with malice, fraud and guile
The sacred enzymes of a world gone bad.
The hoof-beats thunder in my ears.
Leave to the councillors the garbage-plot,
The refuse and the greasy tins
Of this slum-culture—these are not
The area where love begins.
The brutal and the vile are set
As watchers at the gate,
But the Blue Horses scream aloud:
A sudden movement shakes the crowd
Stampeded on the hooves of fate.

## New Guinea Lament

Now glowing Venus wakes
On the tumulus of dusk
And the roaming wild-pig shakes
The dead with rooting tusk.

The flying-foxes swarm
In fading orchards of light,
The keeper cannot keep from harm
Fruit stolen in the night.

My love now are you lying
In the mirrors of your sleep
Or do you watch with inward sighing
Earth's hungry shadows creep

On the dreary day's remains?
Desire like a rusty nail
Pierces time's foot until it seems
His aching tread will fail.

## Missa Papae Marcelli

Now Ixion's wheel is stilled
By that pure rejoicing tone;
Sisyphus the adverse-willed
Sits in quiet by his stone;
For in hell, when music sounds,
Spirits leave their barren rounds.

Sexes that were damned in sin
Outwards turn their quenchless eyes
That before were fixed within
On their gnawing miseries;
When music sounds, the glances meet
Gently, and forgo deceit.

Rulers, artists, who were spent
By ambition that proved vain,
Shake the eternal discontent
From their shoulders; and the pain
Ceases to assault its bounds,
Regenerate, when music sounds.

Sabbath on the brows of Dis!
Earth is silent as a bride.
The shining calm parenthesis
Stills the angry worlds outside.
Magog, looming at the gate,
When music sounds, forgets his hate.

## The Death of Chiron

The herdboys shout unseen among the rocks;
Autumn grows colder, and they lead their flocks
From the high pastures down into the plain.
To feel the golden calm I have dragged my pain
Outside the cavern mouth, but still inhale
The smell of sweat and sickness, dung and stale.

The wild bees know the time of dearth has come,
And signal the grim rites of harvest-home
When crumpled bodies of the drones are thrust
Out of the hive and fall into the dust.
The year sinks underground, and with it I
Put off divinity and learn to die.

A son of Time no less than Zeus, I chose
To be the friend of centaurs and all those
Who draw a harsh life from this mountain breast.

183

I tutored many heroes, but loved best
The hardy unheroic simple folk
Who drive their herds and put the ox to yoke.

I taught them spells and simples that could salve
Their peaceful wounds, or help their cows to calve;
Even the village girls would come for charms
To guard against lost love or freckled arms,
Leaving small gifts of honey, eggs, or fruit;
Or sometimes, laughing, would not long dispute

Among the crushed herbs of the cave to measure
What god and beast can bring to country pleasure.
Sometimes in the spring I joined the dance
With hard hooves beating, and the men would prance
In mimic masks to lead the season in;
And what was done those nights was not held sin.

In winter when the owl sat humped with cold
I came down to their firesides and told
Stories of gods and heroes; and often then
Would tell of one who brought down fire to men,
And how, before the Hero sets him free,
Some god must give his immortality

And die: not as the sacred ear of corn
Lies in darkness waiting to be reborn,
But as the dry stalk falls and vanishes.
A dear exchange it seemed—nor did I guess
What hydra-poisoned arrow, from what bow,
Would send me willing to the shades below.

Heracles, saviour of men, sun-like defender,
I watched your youth rise to its noon-splendour
Of clear heroic fire; but feared to see
The fitful presage of that insanity,
When blundering in a dark eclipse you strike
At shadows, killing friend and child alike.

So Linus died, and Eunomus, then all
Your children; and the darkness yet will fall
On others, as it did on me that day
When the odorous wine-cask bred the wild affray
That drove the routed centaurs to my cave;
And I went down to stay your hand and save

The hunted. I saw blind frenzy in your soul
Like shadows wavering in a red-hot coal,
Such as the warriors of Asia feel
But quench their bodies, as men temper steel,
Hissing in the wave. Unchecked you drew
The bowstring taut, and the long arrow flew.

As the devising wasp with darting skill
Thrusts in her sting to paralyse, not kill,
The insect that survives to be the prey
Of her hatched grub when she has flown away,
So did attentive Fate spring forth to guide
The venomed stroke, then vanished satisfied.

Now when the shepherds bring their summer flocks
To the high pasture-ground among the rocks,
They are afraid to come near where I lie.
There is no herb or spell can purify
The inherent hydra; why should I not consent
To free the Titan from his banishment?

Never was earth more radiant than in this
Last autumn gold that I take down to Dis.
I have loved the earth alone, and had no will
To change the measures of its good and ill;
Others give laws and blame, and sit above,
But there were no conditions in my love.

Men will bewail my fate when I am gone
And in it see the pattern of their own:
Their poisoned instinct writhes incurable
Within the ancient cave of touch and smell;
They feel the hydra-taint of guilty care
Rankle their joy and bring them to despair.

But in exchange, instead of plaited straw,
The heavy golden crown of art and law
Will press upon their brows, and in their hand
The imperial builder's dream of stone will stand;
And on the rustic year they will impose
New time, that does not vary as it flows.

Yet their Promethean victories will rise
But as the smoke of nature's sacrifice
Within, without. Everywhere they tread
The beasts will sicken and the desert spread.
Their baffled Hero in his turn will die
Howling in envenomed agony.

I have but little skill of forward sight,
Nor have I overheard in the still night,
As once the Titan did, the singing Fates:
The spirit alone can judge what it creates
And see it to the end. But I must go
Unreconciled into the dark below.

## *Vespers*

The sunlight falling on the nursery floor
No longer brings the picture-books to life.
The blood dries unavenged upon the knife;
The jewelled nightingale will sing no more
To the dead emperor; magic hopes depart.
What tears shall melt the cold glass in my heart?

And was it after all no map of truth,
That land of Snakes and Ladders where we first
Practised the soul's ascent or fell accursed?
Were they deceitful meanings that in youth
Stories and games seemed anxious to impart,
Now fixed unfading in the frozen heart?

No, Wisdom's self has shed the warm salt tears
Which melt the glassy ice; and he has willed
Nothing whatever should be unfulfilled
That childhood promised to my later years;
Only this added, which I could not know,
That first the bitter tears, like his, must flow.

## *To a Dead Bird of Paradise*

Ah, fabulous fancy,
Now cold and forlorn,
Go dwell with the phoenix
And unicorn.

Your opaline plumage,
Deep-burning jewel,
Falls prey to the hand that is
Cunning and cruel.

That grasps at the colour
And blots out the spark—
Why linger? Naught here can
Relumine the dark.

But there your exemplar,
The phoenix, survives
Unheeded, unheeding,
Through myriad lives:

It lives in the light!
It sings in the fire!
Love burns its ecstatic
And redolent pyre.

Ah, fabled and real,
Betrayed and forlorn,
Go dwell with the phoenix
And unicorn.


## New Guinea

(In memory of Archbishop Alain de Boismenu, M.S.C.)

Bird-shaped island, with secretive bird-voices,
Land of apocalypse, where the earth dances,
The mountains speak, the doors of the spirit open,
And men are shaken by obscure trances.

The forest-odours, insects, clouds and fountains
Are like the figures of my inmost dream,
Vibrant with untellable recognition;
A wordless revelation is their theme.

The stranger is engulfed in those high valleys,
Where mists of morning linger like the breath
Of Wisdom moving on our specular darkness.
O regions of prayer, of solitude, and of death!

Life holds its shape in the modes of dance and music,
The hands of craftsmen trace its patternings;
But stains of blood, and evil spirits, lurk
Like cockroaches in the interstices of things.

We in that land begin our rule in courage,
The seal of peace gives warrant to intrusion;
But then our grin of emptiness breaks the skin,
Formless dishonour spreads its proud confusion.

Whence that deep longing for an exorcizer,
For Christ descending as a thaumaturge
Into his saints, as formerly in the desert,
Warring with demons on the outer verge.

Only by this can life become authentic,
Configured henceforth in eternal mode:
Splendour, simplicity, joy—such as were seen
In one who now rests by his mountain road.

ERIC IRVIN

## *Midnight Patrol*

Now as the night treads softly on its way,
And trees review the march-past of the stars,
We stand and hear leaves chatter. Do they say:
'These must be, surely, visitors from Mars?'
For death is cradled in my arms, my belt
Holds bitter fruit for enemies to eat;
While at my back, four aces yet undealt,
Tread riflemen with slow and wary feet.
Tall trees spring from the darknesses that lie
About their base to greet the moon, but we
Shrink from her light for fear the unseen eye
Should mark our shapes merged with a light-splashed tree
And free the lightning that would make us one
With night that never sees a rising sun.


## *Brother Ass*

Old Brother Ass stands mumchance in the sun,
Dreaming the century's dream of easy wealth,
Dreaming the golden prize; then thumbs in stealth
The latest ticket. In his mind this dun,
Black-printed rag hangs gracefully across
Uneven doorways, shutting out the black
Worm-eaten timbers of the past. Its folds
Are tapestried in gold utopian scenes
Wherein the world is his, or not, for toss
Of any coin from out a well-filled sack.

He folds it up. Tomorrow's drawing holds
So much of his real life within its hands
He dare not think an instant more on fate,
Whose end he neither sees nor understands.


Old Brother Ass stands mumchance in the sun
(The years have taught him only how to wait),
Confined within the glasshouse of his means;
Seeing the world outside with eyes that shun
The greater glasshouse round his smaller one.


## *Christmas 1942*

### I

Here's shade and comfort by this towering tree,
Dear Phaedrus, and a breeze to lull our rest.
Here let our thoughts flow undisturbed and free
As flows Laloki. Many sands have run
Since by Ilissus you and I reclined;
And many comrades journeyed to the sun
With whom we have shared everything but death.


### II

I could not speak of them on my return;
I could not bare the wound so closely wrapped
Against corruption by the spoken word;
My smile the dreamer's shield held up to guard
A sense of impotence, a deep despair
Of making 'over here' see 'over there'.

But someone spoke of Damas and Djezzine,
And phrased a pretty speech about Tobruk,
And in a flash the cramped suburban room,
The silly teacups and the linen cloth,
The heartless sympathy of common speech
Moved out beyond the compass of Time's reach:

And I was in a man's world, and the earth
Shook or stood still as we chose to dictate;
And life was ours, and death, and the sweet pain
Of thinking now and then of other days
When we were human beings, sheltered, fed;
The darlings of existence, fancy-led.

## III

Bitterness sways me but a while: is gone,
And I remember mornings such as this
By such a green-banked, slowly-flowing stream
An aeon of experience ago.
Remember, too, a love that down the years
Has mocked me with its echoed might-have-been.

These notes I gather now; all chords resolve
In pointed harmony phrased by despair;
New-cadenced by regrets that rise and fall;
That hint of a solemn pity: and are gone.

# EDGAR HOLT

## *Two Sonnets from a Sequence*

### I

This side of madness, while the flames abate,
They have heaped their small belongings: tears
(Harsh in pain-dry eyes), hunger and hate,
And all their monstrous catalogue of fears.
Death is the least of these—a troubled sleep
Invaded by the memory of pain,
So much, that even those who die still weep,
And bones cry out and sinews are insane.

At night the children dream, clutching the air
With knotted hands. . . . O sweet to dream of hell,
Where fallen angels burn! O sweet to stare,
Sleepbound, on demons! . . . No, their nightmares tell
The day's tale over, and they run from men,
They run, they run, until they wake again.

### II

Under the midnight's iron rain, under
The ground, under the broken wall and arch,
And the fallen city, there's no room for wonder.
Love is a moment stolen from the march—
The other side of killing, lust that cleaves,
A dry fulfilment of despair, the splinter
Piercing the heart. Its bitter warmth deceives
As cruelly as a lonely sun in winter.

O

He has no time to learn love's alphabet,
No time to wipe the murder from his eyes.
It is enough that he and she are met,
Alive. No rapture here, no strange surprise—
Only a fierce and brutal will to feel,
Kisses that bleed and lips as hard as steel.

## J. S. MANIFOLD

### Fife Tune

(For Sixth Platoon 308th I.T.C.)

One morning in spring
We marched from Devizes
All shapes and all sizes,
Like beads on a string,
But yet with a swing
We trod the bluemetal
And full of high fettle
We started to sing.

She ran down the stair
A twelve-year-old darling
And laughing and calling
She tossed her bright hair;
Then silent to stare
At the men flowing past her—
There were all she could master
Adoring her there.

It's seldom I'll see
A sweeter or prettier,
I doubt we'll forget her
In two years or three,
And lucky he'll be
She takes for a lover
While we are far over
The treacherous sea.


## *Suburban Lullaby*

Fear the lights that cross the street,
Fear the blackout shadows grim,
Fear the bobby on his beat,
Fear the one that watches him:
   Fear the shock when they collide;
   Hurry, hurry home and hide.

Fear the lifting of the bolt;
Fear the fingers at the door:
Friendly hands may thumb a Colt,
Friendly things are friends no more.
   Voices crack that cry 'All's well'.
   Creep to bed and dream of hell.

History naked rides the sky;
Can you take him by the name?
Is there time to justify?
Is there time to start again?
   Dare to hold or dare let go,
   What abysses gape below!

# The Tomb of Lt John Learmonth, A.I.F.

'At the end on Crete he took to the hills, and said he'd fight it out with only a revolver. He was a great soldier . . .'

*One of his men in a letter*

This is not sorrow, this is work: I build
A cairn of words over a silent man,
My friend John Learmonth whom the Germans killed.

There was no word of hero in his plan;
Verse should have been his love and peace his trade,
But history turned him to a partisan.

Far from the battle as his bones are laid
Crete will remember him. Remember well,
Mountains of Crete, the Second Field Brigade!

Say Crete, and there is little more to tell
Of muddle tall as treachery, despair
And black defeat resounding like a bell;

But bring the magnifying focus near
And in contempt of muddle and defeat
The old heroic virtues still appear.

Australian blood where hot and icy meet
(James Hogg and Lermontov were of his kin)
Lie still and fertilize the fields of Crete.

\*        \*        \*

Schoolboy, I watched his ballading begin:
Billy and bullocky and billabong,
Our properties of childhood, all were in.

I heard the air though not the undersong,
The fierceness and resolve; but all the same
They're the tradition, and tradition's strong.

Swagman and bushranger die hard, die game,
Die fighting, like that wild colonial boy—
Jack Dowling, says the ballad, was his name.

He also spun his pistol like a toy,
Turned to the hills like wolf or kangaroo,
And faced destruction with a bitter joy.

His freedom gave him nothing else to do
But set his back against his family tree
And fight the better for the fact he knew

He was as good as dead. Because the sea
Was closed and the air dark and the land lost,
'They'll never capture me alive', said he.

*　　*　　*

That's courage chemically pure, uncrossed
With sacrifice or duty or career,
Which counts and pays in ready coin the cost

Of holding course. Armies are not its sphere
Where all's contrived to achieve its counterfeit;
It swears with discipline, it's volunteer.

I could as hardly make a moral fit
Around it as around a lightning flash.
There is no moral, that's the point of it.

No moral. But I'm glad of this panache
That sparkles, as from flint, from us and steel,
True to no crown nor presidential sash

Nor flag nor fame. Let others mourn and feel
He died for nothing: nothings have their place.
While thus the kind and civilized conceal

This spring of unsuspected inward grace
And look on death as equals, I am filled
With queer affection for the human race.


## JUDITH WRIGHT

### *The Company of Lovers*

We meet and part now over all the world.
We, the lost company,
take hands together in the night, forget
the night in our brief happiness, silently.
We who sought many things, throw all away
for this one thing, one only,
remembering that in the narrow grave
we shall be lonely.

Death marshals up his armies round us now.
Their footsteps crowd too near.
Lock your warm hand above the chilling heart
and for a time I live without my fear.
Grope in the night to find me and embrace,
for the dark preludes of the drums begin,
and round us, round the company of lovers,
Death draws his cordons in.

198

## *Bullocky*

Beside his heavy-shouldered team,
thirsty with drought and chilled with rain,
he weathered all the striding years
till they ran widdershins in his brain:

till the long solitary tracks,
etched deeper with each lurching load,
were populous before his eyes,
and fiends and angels used his road.

All the long straining journey grew
a mad apocalyptic dream,
and he old Moses, and the slaves
his suffering and stubborn team.

Then in his evening camp beneath
the half-light pillars of the trees,
he filled the steepled cone of night
with shouted prayers and prophecies,

while past the camp-fire's crimson ring
the star-struck darkness cupped him round,
and centuries of cattlebells
rang with their sweet uneasy sound.

Grass is across the waggon-tracks,
and plough strikes bone beneath the grass,
and vineyards cover all the slopes
where the dead teams were used to pass.

O vine, grow close upon that bone
and hold it with your rooted hand.
The prophet Moses feeds the grape,
and fruitful is the Promised Land.


## Woman to Man

The eyeless labourer in the night,
the selfless, shapeless seed I hold,
builds for its resurrection-day—
silent and swift and deep from sight
foresees the unimagined light.

This is no child with a child's face;
this has no name to name it by:
yet you and I have known it well.
This is our hunter and our chase,
the third who lay in our embrace.

This is the strength that your arm knows,
the arc of flesh that is my breast,
the precise crystals of our eyes.
This is the blood's wild tree that grows
the intricate and folded rose.

This is the maker and the made;
this is the question and reply;
the blind head butting at the dark,
the blaze of light along the blade.
Oh hold me, for I am afraid.

## Woman's Song

O move in me, my darling,
for now the sun must rise;
the sun that will draw open
the lids upon your eyes.

O wake in me, my darling.
The knife of day is bright
to cut the thread that binds you
within the flesh of night.

Today I lose and find you
whom yet my blood would keep—
would weave and sing around you
the spells and songs of sleep.

None but I shall know you
as none but I have known;
yet there's a death and a maiden
who wait for you alone;

so move in me, my darling,
whose debt I cannot pay.
Pain and the dark must claim you,
and passion and the day.

## Legend

The blacksmith's boy went out with a rifle
and a black dog running behind.
Cobwebs snatched at his feet,
rivers hindered him,

thorn-branches caught at his eyes to make him blind
and the sky turned into an unlucky opal,
but he didn't mind.
I can break branches, I can swim rivers, I can stare out any
    spider I meet
said he to his dog and his rifle.

The blacksmith's boy went over the paddocks
with his old black hat on his head.
Mountains jumped in his way,
rocks rolled down on him,
and the old crow cried, You'll soon be dead!
And the rain came down like mattocks.
But he only said
I can climb mountains, I can dodge rocks, I can shoot an old
    crow any day,
and he went on over the paddocks.

When he came to the end of the day the sun began falling.
Up came the night ready to swallow him,
like the barrel of a gun,
like an old black hat,
like a black dog hungry to follow him.
Then the pigeon, the magpie and the dove began wailing
and the grass lay down to pillow him.
His rifle broke, his hat blew away and his dog was gone
and the sun was falling.

But in front of the night the rainbow stood on the mountain,
just as his heart foretold.
He ran like a hare,
he climbed like a fox,
he caught it in his hands, the colours and the cold—

like a bar of ice, like the column of a fountain,
like a ring of gold.
The pigeon, the magpie and the dove flew up to stare,
and the grass stood up again on the mountain.

The blacksmith's boy hung the rainbow on his shoulder
instead of his broken gun.
Lizards ran out to see,
snakes made way for him,
and the rainbow shone as brightly as the sun.
All the world said, Nobody is braver, nobody is bolder,
nobody else has done
anything to equal it. He went home as easy as could be,
with the swinging rainbow on his shoulder.

## *The Ancestors*

That stream ran through the sunny grass so clear—
more polished than dew is, all one lilt of light.
We found our way up to the source, where stand
the fern-trees locked in endless age
under the smothering vine and the trees' night.

Their slow roots spread in mud and stone,
and in each notched trunk shaggy as an ape
crouches the ancestor, the dark bent foetus;
unopened eyes, face fixed in unexperienced sorrow,
and body contorted in the fern-tree's shape.

That sad, pre-history, unexpectant face—
I hear the answering sound of my blood, I know
these primitive fathers waiting for rebirth,

these children not yet born—the womb holds so
the moss-grown patience of the skull,
the old ape-knowledge of the embryo.

Their silent sleep is gathered round the spring
that feeds the living, thousand-lighted stream
up which we toiled into this timeless dream.

## The Harp and the King

Old king without a throne,
the hollow of despair
behind his obstinate unyielding stare
knows only, God is gone;
and, fingers clenching on his chair,
feels night and the soul's terror coming on.

Bring me that harp, that singer. Let him sing.
Let something fill the space inside the mind,
that's a dry stream-bed for the flood of fear.
Song's only sound; but it's a lovely sound,
a fountain through the drought. Bring David here,
said the old frightened king.

Sing something. Comfort me.
Make me believe the meaning in the rhyme.
The world's a traitor to the self-betrayed;
but once I thought there was a truth in time,
while now my terror is eternity.
So do not take me outside time.
Make me believe in my mortality,
since that is all I have, the old king said.

I sing the praise of time, the harp replied:
the time of aching drought when the black plain
cannot believe in roots or leaves or rain.
Then lips crack open in the stone-hard peaks,
and rock begins to suffer and to pray,
when all that lives has died
and withered in the wind and blown away,
and earth has no more strength to bleed.

I sing the praise of time and of the rain—
the word creation speaks.
Four elements are locked in time;
the sign that makes them fertile is the seed,
and this outlasts all death and springs again,
the running water of the harp-notes cried.

But the old king sighed obstinately,
How can that comfort me?
Night and the terror of the soul come on,
and out of me both water and seed have gone.
What other generations shall I see?
But make me trust my failure and my fall,
said the sad king, since these are now my all.

I sing the praise of time, the harp replied.
In time we fail, alone with hours and tears,
ruin our followers and traduce our cause,
and give our love its last and fatal hurt.
In time we fail and fall.
In time the company even of God withdraws
and we are left with our own murderous heart.

Yet it is time that holds,
somewhere although not now,
the peal of trumpets for us; time that bears,
made fertile even by these tears,
even by this darkness, even by this loss,
incredible redemptions—hours that grow,
as trees grow fruit, in a blind holiness,
the truths unknown, the loves unloved by us.


But the old king turned his head sullenly.
How can that comfort me,
who see into the heart as deep as God can see?
Love's sown in us; perhaps it flowers; it dies.
I failed my God and I betrayed my love.
Make me believe in treason; that is all I have.


This is the praise of time, the harp cried out—
that we betray all truths that we possess.
Time strips the soul and leaves it comfortless
and sends it thirsty through a bone-white drought.
Time's subtler treacheries teach us to betray.
What else could drive us on our way?
Wounded we cross the desert's emptiness
and must be false to what would make us whole.
For only change and distance shape for us
some new tremendous symbol for the soul.

## DAVID CAMPBELL

### *Soldier's Song*

Though I march until I drop
And my bed is sand,
I have filled the desert's cup;
Harvested its land.
This is the song of the desert wind,
From the sphinx it blows:
The Murray's source is in the mind
And at a word it flows.

Though I climb the bitter rock,
Jungle for a bed,
I can muster such a flock
As never Falkiner bred.
This is the song of the tropic wind
Where the giant storm grows:
The Murray's source is in the mind
And at a word it flows.

### *Men in Green*

Oh, there were fifteen men in green,
Each with a tommy-gun,
Who leapt into my plane at dawn;
We rose to meet the sun.

We set our course towards the east
And climbed into the day
Till the ribbed jungle underneath
Like a giant fossil lay.

We climbed towards the distant range
Where two white paws of cloud
Clutched at the shoulders of the pass;
The green men laughed aloud.

They did not fear the ape-like clouds
That climbed the mountain crest
And hung from twisted ropes of air
With thunder in their breast.

They did not fear the summer's sun,
In whose hot centre lie
A hundred hissing cannon shells
For the unwatchful eye.

And when on Dobadura's field
We landed, each man raised
His thumb towards the open sky;
But to their right I gazed.

For fifteen men in jungle green
Rose from the kunai grass
And came towards the plane. My men
In silence watched them pass;
It seemed they looked upon themselves
In Time's prophetic glass.

Calm on the yellowing page was Sarah's name,
How, her poor shift for shroud,
She was buried to the kind words of Andrew Love—
(First pastor here, and she his pastoral grieve)—
Sarah Lorton, with her death upon her.

'By drowning, a poor female, aged forty.'
But she was younger—thirty-three—
When she slipped from the bank below the immigrant
      barracks,
With a pitcher to fill at Barwon Breakwater,
That hot Thursday in December eighteen-forty.

But no Ophelia in long purples palled,
With noble youth to garland her still beauty,
She floated down the stream remembering
The tears of little things that make us glad—
The lacquer on a cat-faced button box,
Red velvet curtains, yellow kitchen clocks—
While black swans, plumed and stately on the green,
Were Caroline Newcomb, Charlotte Fisher, riding
Down the flanks of Strawberry Hill to dole out tracts
To the brickmakers, blue in their stubborn marsh clay.
('To make them good, and keep the drink away.'
O sidelong gait that after grog shop shuts,
Stumps slugfoot home to iceberg eyes and hearts!)
The stench of mutton-fat, the barracks fires,
Sealed off the river mist on Sarah's day.

Though voice to voice rings down the hollow years
Always death leaps the threshold where our ears
Take over from the past.
Almost I hear them now:—

225

Q

David Fisher, testy when old because no one
Could well remember all that he had seen;
Andrew Love, whose voice was all affection,
Most dear in consolation;
And Fyans, with the bite of Ulster mulled
By twenty years of warm colonial days.

This side of life she had no time to spare;
But there—
Where Sarah's gone—
No conscience tolls a passing-bell for pleasure.
They pluck blanched flowers in the valley of the moon,
Sarah Lorton and her death together.


## Three Trees at Solstice

Comes with autumn the spent moment,
When, polarized to stillness,
The soul thereafter waits on death
As oaks on winter,
As oaks by winter water.
So stands the sun for springing and failing time;
And a life ending is less than a stream failing
Until, sunk deep in a white meander—
Black clouds come down like swans at brood,
And flows again the white water.

The silver tree of the stream
Fails not for the sea,
Nor for thirst-hewn rocks of the valley;
But fails the red, bright tree
In each man's breast—

Drooping to winter's rest;
Fails the yellow tree
Of each day's light—
Fails from sight,
Fails in the west.


MAX HARRIS

## Lullaby

Girl with eyes like dying flowers,
come near and close them and shut out
the elegant spring. You have lived hours
on the moon's lips among night flowers.

If your hand is cold and wet
and your thoughts a cruel cage
let your body stretch to me and set
its marble like disaster in my flesh.

Now your golden hair lies dead
and your arms, so white and brown.
The thorn and the storm your eyes have shed
and they are in me and you are dead.


## Martin Buber in the Pub

My friends are borne to one another
By their lack of something to say;
The weight of inward thought is lifted
And they float to each other
Like paper darts: they offer the salt of themselves
Arab-like in hotels,

Humbler than they would have you believe.
Humanity is the smallest coin for tipping.
Allen relates a host of grandiose lies . . .
These are the wafers of our religion.
Barnes is the butt of malice,
An unmysterious drinking of the blood . . .
And the seas may boil outside. No doubt they do.
But we are in a silence of some sort,
Exchanging shells, which placed against the ear,
Occasionally echo the throbbing of a heart.

GEOFFREY DUTTON

## *Nightflight and Sunrise*

The flux of night is power and will, slid
Like a coined sun into the dark horizon.
Shadows hollow out the convex earth
Of mystery, till the hills
Of the knuckles are one with the mountains of the moon.

'Who can distinguish darkness from the soul?'
The explorer lightless beyond the wings, by red
And green exalted and tore out the eyes
Of cat and fox. The body
Was entered, as will is seldom, by the soul.

Riding the groundswell of the dark is the impulse
Born of love, whose only maps of light
Are a green beam, wind in a flame's motion
Of flares that sit like jewels

While bushfires on a fox's brush race hills
And hounds in air. Through their consuming blows
The wind of planets, cut keener past the cheek
Than knives of light along the unseen roads.
The face by the fire, shadowed like a pirate,
Holds life in eyes that judge,
Eased back and ruddered to the fatal ground.


But the armoured sun infiltrates the vast dark miles,
Will and its body spring forward like shadows,
And the airman sees behind the secret hedge
The movements of the morning.
The flux of night becomes the will to live


Behind a death whirled more sudden than scythe
In mist of a propeller, fledged gently
In the veiled hills and creeks veined like a walnut.
The flame in the black well
Is gone. But the airman's hand stroked skin


Of the cosmic heart and counted the beats from day.
He airborne and alone was stressed of stars
And entered the source of all activity.
As shadows leap away
From light, so with their substance he awaits the night.

## *A Prisoner Freed*

The wind slammed shut the door and he remembered
The last bolt home, final clang of despair,
Saw stone rise through the carpet and the moon
Lie barred across the floor. Suddenly he knew,
Only memory can lay bare actuality
And he who shuts his eyes alone can see.

Through the dissolving walls he felt the night
Fall from him, come down five sides of air
And lock him in ennui, softly as a fog,
With death for lover in his waiting bed.
The vacant moving light is a clock of comfort
And points the hunger in satiety

That sees him shuffle uneasily into the future
Like a drunkard into a church. The actual hour
Of love alone is apprehended
As a triumph and a death, the sour remainder
Is the day of bone and blood trying to fight
With hand and eye the unseen enemy of the mind.

Now a kindly jailer turns him
On a key of days, a padlock on the mind
That lies most heavy as intangible,
Smiling that his is the subtlest captivity being free,
Linked on an unseen leash like gravity
To earth, and death still virgin on the sheet.

## *January*

In summer, when the hills are blond
O dark-haired girl with wave-wet ankles
Bare your skin to the sun and to me.
All summer go brown, go salt by the sea.

O dark-haired girl stay close to me
As grass that shivers on the hill's hot flank
Or your spine that trembles under my hand;
The pale grass is dead, but not so the sea.

Across the paddocks stooks and bales
In separate civilizations stand
Like tribesmen's tents and townsmen's cities,
While a dark girl swims in distant seas.

The sun's blond fire turns red and black,
A horrible army runs through hay
By flank of hill through hair of tree
And the ashes fall upon the sea.

Stook-tents, bale-cities all fall down
And fences keep the dead stock back.
O dark-haired girl, stay close to me.
All summer go brown, go salt by the sea.

FRANCIS WEBB

## For My Grandfather

When the ropes droop and loosen, and the gust
Piecemeal upon a widening quietness fails,
Fail breath and spirit; against the bony mast
Work in like skin the frayed and slackened sails.
In the green lull where ribs and keel lie wrecked,
Wrapped in the sodden, enigmatic sand,
Things that ache sunward, seaward, with him locked,
Tug at the rigging of the dead ship-lover's hand.
Though no wind's whitening eloquence may fill
Drowned canvas with the steady bulge of breath,
Doubling for past, for future, are never still
The bones ambiguous with life and death.

Dusk over Bradley's Head: a feeble gull
Whose sinking body is the past at edge
Of form and nothing: here the beautiful
Letona gybes, off the spray-shaken ledge.
And to those years, dusk comes but as a rift
In the flesh of sunlight, closed by memory:
Shells stir in the pull of water, lift
Fragile and holy faces to the sky.
My years and yours are scrawled upon this air
Rapped by the gavel of my living breath:
Rather than time upon my wrist I wear
The dial, the four quarters of your death.

## *The Gunner*

When the gunner spoke in his sleep the hut was still,
Uneasily strapped to the reckless wheel of his will;
Silence, humble, directionless as fog,
Lifted, and minutes were rhythmical on the log;

While slipstream plucked at a wafer of glass and steel,
Engines sliced and scooped at the air's thin wall,
And those dim spars dislodged from the moon became
Red thongs of tracer whipping boards aflame.

Listening, you crouched in the turret, watchful and taut
—*Bogey two thousand, skipper, corkscrew to port*—
Marvellous, the voice: driving electric fires
Through the panel of sleep, the black plugs, trailing wires.

The world spoke through its dream, being deaf and blind,
Its words were those of the dream, yet you might find
Forgotten genius, control, alive in this deep
Instinctive resistance to the perils of sleep.

## *Laid Off*

### I. *The Bureau, and Later*

Outside the Bureau all the trams and trains
Prattled securely, with us out of air
To ply like bits of refuse among drains
Nudging each other nastily when it rains.

Only the suck or slap of rubber sole
At marble was our case and hearing. Spare
Butts, down to earth, drafted one smoky scroll
For factory, office, wharf, and police patrol.

I pitied the man behind the counter, who'd
Hear us be cruelly serious, hear us swear,
Be funny, No-speak-English—see us bowed
Under the weight of tools to make him God.

Later:—this swine with platitudinous
Squeaks of his oily leather-bottomed chair
Makes up his mouth to tell me less and less
And plays at being Satan, with more success.

To the most dangerous driver, righteous heat,
Our traffic-lights are neither here nor there.
I stare at the pock-marked baby while I eat
And walk past the blind mouth-organist on the street.

## II. *Hard-luck Story*

'Yes, this is the stop for Central. Yes, right here.
Cold weather? Right, I'll try a tailor-made'—
Breaking the ice is moving mountains, sheer
Bravado if there's no time for a prayer.

Frayed eyelids button on to me; this thin
Lip of the cold snap will not have me wade
Or even pet my carefully nourished skin
To reassure it before plunging in.

234

Taxes and breadless children swim or drown
Without mercy inside his overcoat. Afraid?
So I am—but citizens pay to see again
A great dramatist's aquarium of pain.

His bony, dickering, artist's hands attach
Years to my ears; from their ice-box of shade
Castles crane forward, puff themselves up, and watch
For the foolhardy twinkle of my match.

## Morgan's Country

This is Morgan's country: now steady, Bill
(Stunted and grey, hunted and murderous).
Squeeze for the first pressure. Shoot to kill.

*Five*: a star dozing in its cold cavern.
*Six*: first shuffle of boards in the cold house.
And the sun lagging on seven.

The grey wolf at his breakfast. He cannot think
Why he must make haste, unless because their eyes
Are poison at every well where he might drink.

Unless because their gabbling voices force
The doors of his grandeur, first terror, then only hate.
Now terror again. Dust swarms under the doors.

Ashes drift on the dead-sea shadow of his plate.
Why should he heed them? What to do but kill
When his angel howls, when the sounds reverberate

In the last grey pipe of his brain? At the window sill
A blowfly strums on two strings of air:
Ambush and slaughter tingling against the lull.

But the Cave, his mother, is close beside his chair,
Her sunless face scribbled with cobwebs, bones
Rattling in her throat as she speaks. And there

The stone Look-out, his towering father, leans
Like a splinter from the seamed palm of the plain.
Their counsel of thunder arms him. A threat of rain.

*Seven*: and a blaze fiercer than the sun.
The wind struggles in the arms of the starved tree:
The temple breaks on a threadbare mat of grass.

*Eight*: even under the sun's trajectory
This country looks grey, hunted and murderous.

# From *A View of Montreal*

## I. *Cartier at St Malo*

At a certain time in life it becomes essential
To worry about St Malo. Novelty is dangerous:
The white antlers of the floe; Belle Isle in ruins—
Collisions of stone and spray—yet abiding, the pillar
And surly station of disorder.
If hollow-cheeked Anticosti
Should come too often, like a waterfall in sleep,
Opening and closing his senseless eyes, wagging his silver

Dankness of hair (this prophet convulsed) and whistling
Directions to the wind through his wicked shining teeth:
Well, we might come to take him for a roadstead light.
Moreover there is little genuine merit in dying
Of scurvy among barbarians. Suppose that a fisherman
Falls to his death in our natural, antique waters:
What consolations, what golden devices of usage
As he cries at the masthead, wandering footloose, a moment
Abandons himself to the vague forests of air,
Strikes cleanly, and is not wasted! (Indeed, with the feeding
Habits of fish . . . but this is the jest of a veteran.)
He is not of our knowledge, true. He is dead, he is spent,
But an image flowers on this sky and this casual water,
These arbours of order. Our unease, but our exaltation;
Of winter, and radiant; of death, and the marriage-bed.
A girl weeps—but candles enfeature the faces
Of the Saints, but the old bells
Assault and transfigure our whole rich foreshores of silence.

It is to this we have come as the husbandman
Retired with his new, strange bounty of contemplation:
To the mild ways of the coastal sun, to the waves
Docile yet proud as sheaves, tossing their heavy
Glittering heads, and winnowed upon the Sillon.
This never-to-be-spoiled acreage! Others will store
Against our winters its grey bundles of faggots—
The mackerel, John Dory in his crushed mail—
When ships are byred on the shipway.
      And whence are we come?
Strictly speaking, from nowhere. Here is St Malo:
Will you once breathe St Malo
And say there is another air? or say (as a man of discernment)
That childhood is *there*, age *there*, and between is anything?

Confronting the brawny angel of the storm, contending
With the hideous moccasined runner, perhaps I strove
Only for this: that sleep become a haspless door,
As now—a wakefulness. Catherine beside me is quiet;
In this temperate swaying of time, cajolement of passion,
We do not strain to each other:
I am not sailing away tomorrow morning.


But these, the newcomers, up at the crack of dawn,
Their faces as the first light vital, various as towns,
Serene in a stance, or perishing nobly
On the world's most foreign, most slippery ledge (while always
The Court and their sweethearts are somehow close by to
    observe them)—
These I must teach. I say to them, they were better
To lay all petitions on the sure prayer-wheel of the compass
Rather than on the omen or the intention,
As for instance St Elmo's eaglet of fire in the shrouds
Or a sleeping sailor's revelation of landfall.
But remains the white tower of our Service
Whereto all words must aspire; therefore, in concluding,
I counsel them not to belittle the good intention:
For while thirst is a rasp whetted on the bitter
Coarse salt of the sea, while the shark's tooth is a ribbon
Of candid and vicious fire, while hunger and disease
Are, when we come to them, pain and there is nothing
Nothing but pain, neither truth nor good nor evil
In fifty worlds—still beyond these worlds is another.
Let a ship be taken by the ice, squeezed in the scrawny
Fingers of the frozen element, clasped, and racked, and
    splintered,
Driven like a living nail into the heaving bloodless
Face of the cold and clenched there: yet will come back

A Word or a Name.
        If merely a piece of wreckage,
Troubling, shifting in its marble, working like a statue
But cause of its own creation:
Tilting and turning downward among the vigilant
Tapering eyes of the dead, past the locked wheel
And lashings derisive of north and south: thence upward.
In the sun's circles and torrents a seabird
Rapt and lighted and moving,
In the storm marred and perplexed, unresting at the seven
Beaches of sin, nor turning back at the blasphemous
Mirage, the Gates of Herakles swinging outward,
It will come home to us. The more to be marvelled at
For its drapings of terror.
        It is with these words
I cancel myself: irony were a sacrilege,
It is here they take fire, speak loudly, brush me aside,
They burn, their wild humours
Come to the boil in them: they *must* see the King!


In the gale of illusion will march the honest tree,
Self-flagellant, murmuring
Against its gift, the knowing, the queer science—
Mortality, an ague rocking to the root.
On the morrow, mortality is strength. I have known them
    stir me:
St Malo a falsehood; nothing truthful but the green
Loitering disconsolate wind-crossed figure of the sea
In an old archway; nothing to seek but the Saguenay,
Myth of jewels and miles, fact of murder and deceit;
Nothing enduring but Hochelaga, the village
Where our language was wrenched by the red screeching
    birds.

Then, rubbing at starlight, the mast of an anchored ship
Twitches—these tiny movements of peace; then dawn,
Lover, discoverer, charts our St Malo with wakening
Legends and lights; and return is out of the question.

## Five Days Old

Christmas is in the air.
You are given into my hands
Out of quietest, loneliest lands.
My trembling is all my prayer.
To blown straw was given
All the fullness of Heaven.

The tiny, not the immense,
Will teach our groping eyes.
So the absorbed skies
Bleed stars of innocence.
So cloud-voice in war and trouble
Is at last Christ in the stable.

Now wonderingly engrossed
In your fearless delicacies,
I am launched upon sacred seas,
Humbly and utterly lost
In the mystery of creation,
Bells, bells of ocean.

Too pure for my tongue to praise,
That sober, exquisite yawn
Or the gradual, generous dawn
At an eyelid, maker of days:
To shrive my thought for perfection
I must breathe old tempests of action

For the snowflake and face of love,
Windfall and word of truth,
Honour close to death.
O eternal truthfulness, Dove,
Tell me what I hold—
Myrrh? Frankincense? Gold?

If this is man, then the danger
And fear are as lights of the inn,
Faint and remote as sin
Out here by the manger.
In the sleeping, weeping weather
We shall all kneel down together.

## Harry

It's the day for writing that letter, if one is able,
And so the striped institutional shirt is wedged
Between this holy holy chair and table.
He has purloined paper, he has begged and cadged
The bent institutional pen,
The ink. And our droll old men
Are darting constantly where he weaves his sacrament.

Sacrifice? Propitiation? All are blent
In the moron's painstaking fingers—so painstaking.
His vestments our giddy yarns of the firmament,
Women, gods, electric trains, and our remaking
Of all known worlds—but not yet
Has our giddy alphabet
Perplexed his priestcraft and spilled the cruet of innocence.

We have been plucked from the world of commonsense,
Fondling between our hands some shining loot,
Wife, mother, beach, fisticuffs, eloquence,
As the lank tree cherishes every distorted shoot.
What queer shards we could steal
Shaped him, realer than the Real:
But it is no goddess of ours guiding the fingers and the thumb.

She cries: *Ab aeterno ordinata sum.*
He writes to the woman, this lad who will never marry.
One vowel and the thousand laborious serifs will come
To this pudgy Christ, and the old shape of Mary.
Before seasonal pelts and the thin
Soft tactile underskin
Of air were stretched across earth, they have sported and are
one.

Was it then at this altar-stone the mind was begun?
The image besieges our Troy. Consider the sick
Convulsions of movement, and the featureless baldy sun
Insensible—sparing that compulsive nervous tic.
Before life, the fantastic succession,
An imbecile makes his confession,
Is filled with the Word unwritten, has almost genuflected.

Because the wise world has for ever and ever rejected
Him and because your children would scream at the sight
Of his mongol mouth stained with food, he has resurrected
The spontaneous though retarded and infantile light.
Transfigured with him we stand
Among walls of the no-man's-land
While he licks the soiled envelope with a lover's caress

Directing it to the House of no known address.


VINCENT BUCKLEY

## Father and Son

The tall wheels grate into the miles
The jinker takes to Cherokee.
I sit perched on a stumble; he
Pretends a song, or quaintly smiles;
Our minds, unmeeting, still agree
To mark each other's loving wiles.
Of the same bone and temperament,
We differ in the powers spent
To come to this wrenching peace again:
Two small, self-wounding, fearful men
Riding on rock, on flint, on knives,
Who travel from their cramping lives.
What shall I speak of? The bland earth?
Question a dog's or kinsman's worth?
If mind falters in what I say,
Love cannot guard the entered way:
'It's black Orangemen own these farms,
Crushing us with their pious arms.'

*'Ah, they're no worse than ever our own,*
*Who'd strip you to the shuddering bone*
*And then use that to fertilize*
*The sullen land beyond that rise,*
*Making their life a bloody war.*
*You're better out of it where you are.*
*I curse the day I saw this place.'*
The spokes are webbed with light; I face
Patiently such words as these
And wait, preparing words of ease,
But fail: '*Ah, we're a spendthrift lot.*'
The soft hair growing coarse, the hot
Veins beating in the Irish head,
And the limbs terrified of death?
*'And yet with a quick meanness, too,*
*To hoard a pound and still undo*
*All that we had thought was ours.'*
Self-pity could go on for hours.
We meet only in silence, stress
Each other with our separateness.
Yes, I can glimpse in what we say
Our impotence in this modern day,
The love of everything contrary
Our family motto still preserves,
*Nec timide nec temere.*
Meaning: Do everything by halves,
Half-patient, then half-passionate,
Half-soundly loving while we hate,
And, even while the ploughshare steers,
Nothing's completely in control.
*'Still, they were sort of pioneers.'*
Broke land, at least, and backs, at least;
I thought to pioneer a soul,

244

Your soul and mine, from the wretched past
Brought to a common pitch at last.
And 'Summer will be bad, I think.'
'*Well, what we need is a bloody drink.*'
Uncertain gesturings that track
The five common miles, and back.

## Late Tutorial

The afternoon dark increases with the clock
And shadows greening on the cabinet.
Teacher of youth, and more than half a fool,
How should you catch those shadows in your net?

Outside, the world's late colour calls us home:
Not to the refuge of familiar art
Nor house of settling wood, but to the first
Home, to the savage entry of the heart.

There, where the dry lips are cooled with words
And every hand worships the love it serves,
Perhaps we'll find some comfort: the deep spring
Rising, and soft renewal of the nerves

In poetry with its constant singing mouth.
Open the door, then; numbed with winter air,
They smile, and move inside; the colours fade
Ringing my head; they seat themselves, and stare.

So I must learn that these, the learners, come
To teach me something of my destiny;
That love's not pity, words are not mine alone,
And all are twined on the great central tree.

How shall I answer them, give ultimate name
To the nerves at war, the mind in dishabille?
Better to pace with the slow clock, and teach them
Quibbles with which to meet adversity.

Their thoughts come, slow, from a cold bed. Their needs
Are close to me as the smell of my own flesh.
Their timid guesses grow, soft-fallen seeds,
To grace my mind with pain. And should I say

    'O man is sick, and suffering from the world,
    And I must go to him, my poetry
    Lighting his image as a ring of fire,
    The terrible and only means I have;

    And, yet, I give too much in rhetoric
    What should be moulded with a lifetime's care,
    What peace alone should strike, and hear vibrate
    To the secret slow contraction of the air,'

The talk would die in loud embarrassment,
The books be rustled, and the noses blown
In frenzy of amazement at this short
Still youthful puppet in academic gown.

I cannot, but speak measured foolish words:
Shelley was fitful, Keats a dozing fire.
Pass with the light, poor comrades. You and I
Follow but feebly where our words aspire.

## Secret Policeman

Pledge me: I had the hangman for a father
And for my mother the immortal State;
My playground was the yard beside the limepit,
My playsongs the aftercries of hate.

Admire me: I fill these shining boots,
I am soul expanded to a uniform;
A hired world glitters at my senses,
The smell of blood keeps my bloodstream warm.

Pity me: From a world ruddy with flame
I am tugged in dreams to the first cave again,
And in that humid soil and atmosphere
Lie down each night beside the murdered men.

The dead eyes point the way I go,
The dead hands presage me in air.
I run on shifting pavements, by fired walls
Falling, and weighted lamp-posts everywhere.

## No New Thing

No new thing under the sun:
The virtuous who prefer the dark;
Fools knighted; the brave undone;
The athletes at their killing work;
The tender-hearts who step in blood;
The sensitive paralysed in a mood;

The clerks who rubber-stamp our deaths,
Executors of death's estate;
Poets who count their dying breaths;
Lovers who pledge undying hate;
The self-made and self-ruined men;
The envious with the strength of ten.
They crowd in nightmares to my side,
Enlisting even private pain
In some world-plan of suicide:
Man, gutted and obedient man,
Who turns his coat when he is told,
Faithless to our shining world.
And hard-faced men, who beat the drum
To call me to this Cause or that,
Those heirs of someone else's tomb,
Can't see the sweeter work I'm at,
The building of the honeycomb.


RAY MATHEW

*Young Man's Fancy*

Come tomorrow night,
or don't come ever.
The moon will give light
enough for a lover.

I'll stand in the deep dark
of a gum-tree's shadow,
but you'll find me all right
if you really want to.

But I won't wait long,
You must come if you're coming.
Without talk of wrong
or breakfast at morning.

If they find out
just say you were walking
to see if the night
could stop a head aching.

And don't mention me
because I don't own you.
We just happen to meet;
I don't really know you.

Yes, I want you to come,
with the moon in your hair.
And the moon in your eyes
as you look for me there.

Yes, I want you to come,
but I'll promise you nothing.
And if you're not game
then I still won't be crying.

But come tomorrow night
or don't come ever.
I won't spend two nights
waiting for a lover.

## *The Poems come Easier*

The poems come easier
when you're very tired
with your head on the pillow
so the thoughts can creep.
But the head is heavier,
the pencil bigger,
and the words fall asleep.

The poems come easier
when the heart's a black crow
And your eyes scoop hollows
in the hard earth's glare.
But the thought is self-pity,
the tune monotonous,
and your note-book's not there.

The poems come easier
when your body shouts singing
because you're beside her
though you're miles apart.
But the song is a wild duck
not easy catching,
and it flies to the calm
in the heart of your heart.

But the poems come easiest
when you're really belonging,
and the deep earth and the dark sea
find in you home.

Then the bees that were buzzing
like flies at your eyelids
bring yellow-sun pollen
with song to the comb.


## At a Time

At a time when love and love
was more than I could bear to give
she cried out, 'Then I'm alone,
lonely in the world, alone.'

As I stood beside the bay
that the sun set burning bright
she cried tears into my hand,
all I offered was my hand.

I explained the fact of love,
the minute thing that humans have,
but I stumbled on her name;
confused her own, her own pet-name.

Suddenly, a midnight swan
treading white the water sun
rose up and made his own the air,
truly took the trembling air.

Suddenly, most moved by love
I raised her face to see it move,
and we kissed as lovers kiss.
Why remember more than that?

GWEN HARWOOD

## O Could One Write as One Makes Love

O could one write as one makes love
when all is given and nothing kept,
then language might put by at last
its coy elisions and inept
withdrawals, yield, and yielding cast
aside like useless clothes the crust
of worn and shabby use, and trust

its candour to the urgent mind,
its beauty to the searching tongue.
Safe in the world's great house with all
its loves and griefs, at ease among
its earthly fruits, original
as earth and air, the body learns
peace, while the mind in torment burns

to strip the cloak of daily use
from language. Could one seize and move
the stubborn words to yield and sing,
then one would write as one makes love
and poems and revelations spring
like children from the mind's desire,
original as light and fire.

## Home of Mercy

By two and two the ruined girls are walking
at the neat margin of the convent grass
into the chapel, counted as they pass
by an old nun who silences their talking.

They smooth with roughened hands the clumsy dress
that hides their ripening bodies. Memories burn
like incense as towards plaster saints they turn
faces of mischievous children in distress.

They kneel: time for the spirit to begin
with prayer its sad recourse to dream and flight
from their intolerable weekday rigour.
Each morning they will launder, for their sin,
sheets soiled by other bodies, and at night
angels will wrestle them with brutish vigour.

## Prize-giving

Professor Eisenbart, asked to attend
a girls' school speech night as an honoured guest
and give the prizes out, rudely declined;
but from indifference agreed, when pressed
with dry scholastic jokes, to change his mind,
to grace their humble platform, and to lend

distinction (of a kind not specified)
to the occasion. Academic dress
became him, as he knew. When he appeared
the girls whirred with an insect nervousness,
the Head in humbler black flapped round and steered
her guest, superb in silk and fur, with pride

to the best seat beneath half-hearted blooms
tortured to form the school's elaborate crest.
Eisenbart scowled with violent distaste,
then recomposed his features to their best
advantage: deep in thought, with one hand placed
like Rodin's Thinker. So he watched the room's

mosaic of young heads. Blonde, black, mouse-brown
they bent for their Headmistress' opening prayer.
But underneath a light (no accident
of seating, he felt sure), with titian hair
one girl sat grinning at him, her hand bent
under her chin in mockery of his own.

Speeches were made and prizes given. He shook
indifferently a host of virgin hands.
'*Music!*' The girl with titian hair stood up,
hitched at a stocking, winked at near-by friends,
and stood before him to receive a cup
of silver chased with curious harps. He took

her hand, and felt its voltage fling his hold
from his calm age and power; suffered her strange
eyes, against reason dark, to take his stare
with her to the piano, there to change
her casual schoolgirl's for a master's air.
He forged his rose-hot dream as Mozart told

254

the fullness of all passion or despair
summoned by arrogant hands. The music ended,
Eisenbart teased his gown while others clapped,
and peered into a trophy which suspended
his image upside down: a sage fool trapped
by music in a copper net of hair.

FRANCIS  GEYER  (Gwen Harwood)

## Monday

Kröte sits on the beach at noon
   drinking the blood-red wine.
'O how shall I pluck from air some tune
   to match this life of mine?'

A Council notice close at hand
   says liquor is forbidden.
In a damp hollow in the sand
   he keeps his bottle hidden.

A few young mothers come his way.
   They frown at Kröte, jerking
their children past as if to say
   decent men would be working.

Kröte thinks: If I had a child . . .
   and dreams himself a creature
With smoky hair, whose spirit's wild
   as wind, whose inmost nature

mirrors his love. The crowding gulls
   rise, as a dumpy likeness
Of Kröte's dream, in spectacles,
   stones them. A wave of sickness

shakes him. The child comes close, and hangs
   over him with a grin,
then with her metal spade she bangs
   sharply on Kröte's shin.

Kröte flinches with pain, and scowls.
   'Mädchen, why do you hit me?'
He grabs the lifted spade. She howls
   'Don't let that bad man get me.'

The women turn from their affairs.
   The vicious child lets loose a
torrent of lies. Her mother glares
   at Kröte like Medusa.

'Monster! You filthy pervert!' scream
   the child-envenomed jury;
round his condemned retreat they seam
   the tissue of their fury.

In vain this night will Kröte try
   on the rinsed beach to find
his wine, or lose the thoughts that lie
   like stains upon his mind.

## KATH WALKER

### *Understand, Old One*

Understand, old one,
I mean no desecration
Staring here with the learned ones
At your opened grave.
Now after hundreds of years gone
The men of science coming with spade and knowledge
Peer and probe, handle the yellow bones,
To them specimens, to me
More. Deeply moved am I.

Understand, old one,
I mean no lack of reverence.
It is with love
I think of you so long ago laid here
With tears and wailing.
Strongly I feel your presence very near
Haunting the old spot, watching
As we disturb your bones. Poor ghost,
I know, I know you will understand.

What if you came back now
To our new world, the city roaring
There on the old peaceful camping place
Of your red fires along the quiet water,
How you would wonder
At towering stone gunyas high in air
Immense, incredible;

S

Planes in the sky over, swarms of cars
Like things frantic in flight.
What if you came at night upon these miles
Of clustered neon lights of all colours
Like Christian newly come to his Heaven or Hell
And your own people gone?

Old one of the long ago,
So many generations lie between us
But cannot estrange. Your duty to your race
Was with the simple past, mine
Lies in the present and the coming days.

## COLIN THIELE

### Radiation Victim

Beneath your cooling coverlet you lie,
The unseen fire still burning in your flesh,
Yet all humanity may pass you by
Unheeded while you melt before its flame,
And the slim needles of its secret rays
Drive inwards to incinerate your name.
God, that we should see you slowly burn alive!

This is the stealthy modern way to die:
To take the passive metal in your grip
And unaware set all your hand on fire.
Walk down the street or work your innocent bench,
While the unfelt heat burns slowly to the bone
With flame that no man's artifice can quench.

COLIN THIELE

A fine ghastliness this is to end our days:
An ancient incandescence fanned and freed
To leap the air invisibly until
Each mortal breast, ignited and ablaze,
Shrinks to its blackened ashes silently.
And a strange compassion has macabre birth
Now that the unseen fire may stalk and scorch
Its darting probe through the wide round Earth,
May thrust its flame against our cringing flesh
And make mankind its hideous secret torch.


## TV Viewer in a Midnight Café

In the loud gloom, corridor of noise and darkness,
His face turns upwards, held like a mask to the wall,
Snailed by a dry slime. Before him
His long drink thrusts up its straws like snorkels.
Thick froth and turgid cliché, melted and served as one,
Smoother than ooze, are sucked at and spooned together.

All round him the hulks of his peers hunch—
Mouths munching vacantly or falling open
Moment by moment; the soft cud melts,
The long swallow hangs on the screen's apocalypse.

As green-grey and silver as putrefying flesh
The sickly pallor floods over forehead and hand;
He sits as fixed and unmoving as the unguided blind,
Ravaged by the cold bright infection of our times—
Its sly virus slowly ptomaining his mind.

Yet sweet as a syrup the luring and lingering taste
Still clings to his palate. Like bells in the quiet,
The soda and sentiment, mushed to a sweet-sick paste,
Pour over his world their tender and saccharine flood,
Form the thews of his body, *ersatz* for his soul's hard diet;
Spiritual diabetic, he strides up the night to the morning,
Where only his walk still savours of flesh and blood.

## J. R. ROWLAND

### *At Noosa*

All day the house blooms like a sail
   With air and light
Trembling at anchor on its gaptoothed piles
In a seawind soft as talc that touches and again touches
   Like a sweet mother. Spade and pail
Trip us by open doors, pennies and shells
Scatter on ledges and on windowsills

With combs, my thongs, your lipstick, safetypins.
   Sand in the shower,
Salty towels on the veranda rail.
The worn mirror's bloodshot brown eye
   Shows us each evening darker skins,
Eyes clearer, bleaching hair. Sunstruck we lie
At ease or swim or climb the rocks or play

At sandcastles on the dazzling field
   Of empty beach
Plump as the children's faces, that grow warm
And smooth and simple to the touch as sand.

At dark the children yield
Willingly to sleep, as the sea sound
Builds over the house a temple, round

Columns and low roof, that rise
    Close by our windows, where
The folding surf renews its hiss and crumple
Vague white on white in darkness; till the moon
    Swelling towards fullness like these days
Restores the distance, floods the sky with milk,
The sea with diamond flashes, breathing silk

Scents in our faces. As we find each other
    A child laughs in sleep
And still we have uncounted days, our view
Ends in no cliff, the beach is ours,
    Morning fulfils the stars' pledge of fair weather.
All true; yet items in the full account
Are sandflies, washing-up, mosquitoes, rent,

Three days' rain, and something like a quarrel.
    Lara and Zhivago
Had no children, nor is laundry mentioned
By Lawrence in a similar situation
    With Frieda in the cottage at Thirroul—
It makes a certain difference to the tone.
Exaltation needs to be alone

And art selects; but if we take the whole
    Seldom we shall
Do better, or be better as ourselves.
Be thankful then the mosquitoes were so few
    The time so radiant, that if we did fail
Our failures served to toughen the alloy
As stars give sense to night, or night to day.

## *Seven Days*

Thunder moved in sleep,
Birds dropped from the sky, white-eyed,
Every animal died
The evening of the first day.
Fish curdled the sea
Whales panting on their side
Clogged the uneven tide
The evening of the second day.
On the third day the stars
Darkened, sun and moon
Ended their alternate reign.
The fourth day the last leaf
Perished, herb and seed
Shrivelled from the flayed
Earth. Water and land
Merged on the fifth day, on the sixth
Darkness and light. The seventh
Became a thousand aeons without word.

### BRUCE BEAVER

## *Third Degree*

'Why are you troubled, young man, young man?
Why are you restless, young fellow?'
I know there are ways to plot and plan,
But where's the one to follow?

'Why are you bitter, young blood, young blood?
Why are you chilled, young marrow?'
I know there is bad, I know there is good;
It's the rest that rack and harrow.

'Why are you bursting, young heart, young heart?
What sets your bones a-rattle?'
It's the sight of the slaughterer's reeking cart—
The sound of the moaning cattle.

'Why not relax, young stress, young strain?
Why not be clearer, young reason?'
There's a shower of radioactive rain
Has put out my sun for a season.

'You could be meek, young soul, young soul.
You could be mild, young spirit.'
There will be echoes when I howl—
There will be ears to hear it.

'Best to be still, young idiot.
Best to be wholly silent.'
How else may a nerve-end gauge the rot—
By a way less sure and violent?

'You should lie down, young dog, young cur.
You should be dead and buried.'
I stand up now in my shirt of hair,
Lie naked with the married.

'You have been tried, young criminal.
You have been sentenced justly.'
I will ask pardon of the wall—
Its sockets' tears are grisly.

'You will be lost, young ill-at-ease.
You will be soon forgotten.'
I will be found in memories
That else lie dead and rotten.

'You will be damned, young good as dead.
You will be cursed forever—'
My body will sate you, and my head
Float singing down the river!

## R. A. SIMPSON

## *The Death of the Devil*

The Devil, with a gesture understood
All through damnation, said that, for our good,

He would depart and give away his rule:
Reason wrecked his myth and made him a fool.

We let him go in flames, gigantically
Like factory smoke. When everyone was free

There was rejoicing for awhile. But then
The walls of Hell began to glow again

Because a figure like a mirror rose
In flames, reflecting us in every pose.

Like us, although more rational and wise,
The Devil was reborn without disguise.

Now cold, he rules the pit in which we burn.
Few saw the joke or welcomed his return.

## Park Orator

All questions asked, the final answer's lost
Like men diminishing where paths begin.
The orator now amplifies the cost

Where only paper's blown on lawns, and thin
Dogs speculate. Upon his broken stand,
He waits their ridicule. But dogs can't grin.

Next Sunday, crowds will stay and understand
The speech upon these steps—and quickly cheer
His cause and banishment from every land

Where fools comply with bricks around their fear.
But indiscriminate on daydream grass,
The rubbish left becomes alive and clear:

He finds a legion there that makes new stress
And lets him rise, rehearse what should be said:
This multitude will arm and then oppress.

He must compel again, forgetting dread,
And show the rabble how revolts are won
By prophets who may look towards the sun.
But cleaners come and sweep the crowd instead.

BRUCE DAWE

## The City: Midnight

Out of the sighs and breath of each small citizen
Clasped in his neutral bed with eyelids locked
On the frail Pandora's box of consciousness,

Out of the blind susurrus of limbs
Moving like weeds within sleep's rhythmic waters,
Marked by the metronome of clock and moon,

Out of the shadowy cubes stacked carelessly
On night's blue nursery floor by infant men,
Rises the vast and tremulous O of dreams . . .

    The knitting spider watches from her shelf,
    The vague and changing shapes of furniture wait;
    Now slippered ghosts grope down familiar stairs,

    While from mysterious doorways, very soon,
    The starlit insomniacs toddle, arms extending
    Headless golliwog, frayed teddy, broken drum.

Down the long streets they go; they will not wake;
They will walk miles before they turn back, weary,
Clutching the dolls they could not give away.

Morning again will prise their fingers loose,
And all their playthings crumble into light.

## *Freewill Offering*

Sweetheart, please find herewith
a city gift or two,
the early morning thud
of newspapers on porches,
the yawns in misty mirrors,
milk-bottles' humble dew.


A bouquet of smoke-roses
from all-night factories,
the creaking symphony
of elderly women cleaners
making their devotions on
heroic bended knees.


The first benevolent sparrow
cross-questioning a crumb . . .
In wards where nurses run
civilization's messages
—the squeal of twenty babies
debating why they've come.


I give you, too, the cheeky
vivacity of grass
tickling up the asphalt,
scrawling green on stone,
the brazen gaze of Robert Burns
when pretty women pass.

And peace—such as the sea-gull
knows though bartering blue
of ocean for the sallow
grey of river anchorage,
imperturbably eyeing
oil-slick, floating orange-peel—
I also wish for you.

## And a Good Friday was had by All

You men there, keep those women back
and God Almighty he laid down
on the crossed timber and old Silenus
my offsider looked at me as if to say
nice work for soldiers, your mind's not your own
once you sign that dotted line Ave Caesar
and all that malarkey Imperator Rex

well this Nazarene
didn't make it any easier
really—not like the ones
who kick up a fuss so you can
do your block and take it out on them
                              Silenus
held the spikes steady and I let fly
with the sledge-hammer, not looking
on the downswing trying hard not to hear
over the women's wailing the bones give way
the iron shocking the dumb wood.

Orders is orders, I said after it was over
nothing personal you understand—we had a
drill-sergeant once thought he was God but he wasn't
a patch on you

then we hauled on the ropes
and he rose in the hot air
like a diver just leaving the springboard, arms spread
so it seemed
over the whole damned creation
over the big men who must have had it in for him
and the curious ones who'll watch anything if it's free
with only the usual women caring anywhere
and a blind man in tears.


## To My Typewriter

Be my offsider, quick to make a point
on my behalf, to bark in metal at the least
suspicion of a movement from the shadows . . .
Whatever you are aimed at, shoot to kill;
in this half-world of dubious acts and purposes
there's only room for two: the quick and the dead.
Be bodyguard against the back-street boys,
those cheats and con-men who frequent my skull,
together with their brethren even now
planning break-and-entry from without.

Oiled at all times, may each key await
with patience that remorseless triggering
which is your raison d'être,

            and though Time
should add his crepe-soled menace to the rest,

or try to have me look the other way,
even offering at length to cut me in
on all the easy pickings to be had
—I owe that hoodlum nothing who's grown fat
by leading many an amiable hope of mine,
the worse for liquor, up an unlit lane
and making off with everything he had.

Time, vanity, comfort, the desire for peace
—I've seen the sorry victims of their guile
suffering the sly punishment such thugs
are practised in, the thoughtful way
they have of bashing so no bruises show,
the haemorrhaging that never will quite kill . . .

Against these be my ward, cool Remington,
as far as mortal reflexes allow,
be tense to my ten fingers, brain and heart,
and casual as the asp that took its ease
in Cleopatra's bosom
                              be my deadly.


## CHARLES HIGHAM

### *Rushcutter's Bay*

Wire branches, white as spiders' legs and spare
As starved arms rot below the summer vine.
The round moon sits upon the chimney pot
Smiling a deathly smile.
                              Upon the ground
Shred grass, chopped insects, and the humming motors

That chew the spring's long labours. Down below
Black sweatered and blue jeaned the children go.

It is correct. It is correct to say
The ground is full of seed, that plants and limbs
Are full and leaping in a giant season.
Trees, muscled figs from Moreton or skinny
Gums, and the tattered pines that Fletcher knew—
All have fat roots inside the shifting soil
Half sand half earth, untouched by human toil.

The weather shifts each day; nothing ever settles,
Rain crashes, the wind moves across the map,
Reports of drownings. Tin roofs plucked away.
Then for a week the stark and heartless blue.
Impose upon it all you wish to, luck
Or ill-luck, happiness, or despair,
The landscape's level calm resists you there.

In winter, trapped by gloom, we long for this:
The body stripped, sex in blue trunks, the leap
Of water to be carved by pressing shoulders,
Yet now it's here the intellect, a bird
Disgusted by its freedom, tries to fly
Back in the cage to find the door is shut,
Lines of communication are all cut.

So in the sweating and the burnishing
Loaded with lusts we simply take ourselves
To bed at noonday, like the antique gods.
Soundless the sea beats on at the ear's porches;
While knowing ourselves strong we sleep at sand.
And as night comes go see another show,
Stifling together in the spotlight glow.

## EVAN JONES

### *Noah's Song*

The animals are silent in the hold,
Only the lion coughing in the dark
As in my ageing arms once more I fold
My mistress and the mistress of the Ark.

That, the rain, and the lapping of the sea:
Too many years have brought me to this boat
Where days swim by with such monotony,
Days of the fox, the lion, and the goat.

Her breathing and the slow beat of the clock
Accentuate the stillness of the room,
Whose walls and floor and ceiling seem to lock
Into a space as single as the tomb.

A single room set up against the night,
The hold of animals, and nothing more:
For any further world is out of sight—
There are no people, and there is no shore.

True, the time passes in unbroken peace:
To some, no doubt, this Ark would seem a haven.
But all that I can hope for is release.
Tomorrow I'll send out the dove and raven.

## A Voice from Inside

After all the talk was done,
And the questions were dismissed
As merely language with a twist,
I and I were only one.
This wearing body in a sense
Is my true intelligence:
It is past actions that recall
How all flesh gathers to a fall,
And all I do is what is done.
But what I know is not the known.

## VIVIAN SMITH

## Bedlam Hills

Corroded flat as hills allow,
stubbled with stones and brittle weeds,
only the thorn blooms here
and scatters its seeds.

The hills are blank and pale now
beneath the clear and static air.
The landscape is as empty
as a blindman's stare.

Mad Clare, the story tells,
gathered her sticks and pieces here.
Her mind wore on the open rock.
But we forget Clare.

273

Walk over and over the hills of strewn
and fractured rock where the berry
suckles the given stone
and the light breaks clearly.

These are the cold, the worn hills
with madness in their monotone
and emptiness where no life moves
beneath a stone.


## At an Exhibition of Historical Paintings, Hobart

The sadness in the human visage stares
Out of these frames, out of these distant eyes;
the static bodies painted without love
that only lack of talent could disguise.

Those bland receding hills are too remote
Where the quaint natives squat with awkward calm.
One carries a kangaroo like a worn toy;
his axe alert with emphasized alarm.

Those nearer woollen hills are now all streets;
even the water in the harbour's changed.
Much is alike and yet a slight precise
disparity seems intended and arranged—

as in that late pink terrace's façade.
How neat the houses look. How clean each brick.
One cannot say they look much older now,
but somehow more themselves, less accurate.

274

And see the pride in this expansive view:
churches, houses, farms, a prison tower:
a grand gesture like wide-open arms
showing the artist's trust, his clumsy power.

And this much later vision, grander still:
the main street sedate carriages unroll
towards the inappropriate, tentative mountain:
a flow of lines the artist can't control,

the foreground nearly breaks out of its frame
the streets end so abruptly in the water . . .
But how some themes return. A whaling ship.
The last natives. Here that silent slaughter

Is really not prefigured or avoided.
One merely sees a profile, a full face,
a body sitting stiffly in a chair:
the soon-forgotten absence of a race . . .

Album pieces: bowls of brown glazed fruit . . .
I'm drawn back yet again to those few studies
of native women whose long floral dresses
made them first aware of their own bodies.

History has made artists of all these
painters who lack energy and feature.
But how some gazes cling. Around the hall
the pathos of the past, the human creature.

# CHRIS WALLACE-CRABBE

## *Abandoned Cars*

Although the rust-red skeletons survive
Under coiled brambles and their crop of dew
  Old gears do not engage;
While shifts of artifice return to clay
The cohorts of an old green world survive.


Gavotte of pistons, flywheel's pirouette,
These were the pleasantries of man's best friend,
  Abandoned, stiff and cold
Where, tousled by the scrape and brush of scrub,
Our fascinated children pirouette.


Tranquil sedans, rich artefacts that throbbed
With borrowed power in someone's father's time,
  Have come at last to this
Unhallowed ground and this archaic charm.
I saw them here half-shrouded . . . a chord throbbed;


Something responded; something lamented man
Whose poor creations haunt a scene renewed
  By tussock and sharp briar,
Gather a dignity and hunch to earth
In morning light—the infancy of man.

## Going to Sleep

Now switchfall darkness drenches all the room;
Entanglements of line and form are swept
Out of your ken; well-fingered shapes become
The one broad shape of night
And who can tell what sullen rules are kept?

Out there, beyond the cot-bars, what remains?
Wall-paper, rough towels, wooden toys,
Forbidden cupboards and a shattered train—
All these are sunken deep;
No vase can fall, no being makes a noise.

The bars that you can feel enclose a world,
The circumscribed dominion of King Touch.
As blind as Oedipus and strangely cold
You grip your blanket, hear
Far trams, a muffled radio: not much.

A father and a mother drift away.
Tossed on the flux, their independent boats
Eddy and swirl beyond Port Phillip Bay,
Enter the open sea;
Cupped in the blue god's hand their marriage floats.

Withdraw into your blanket. Shut your eyes.
Feckless imagination flirts with death
And must be drowned. Relax and realize
That sun will lick your panes
And white clouds blossom on your morning breath.

RODNEY HALL

## Flight

(For Tom Shapcott)

The unimaginative drowned upon their feet in heavy storms.

To lift the first thick body from the ground,
to rise upon that enemy the storm,
to turn remembrance into second-sight,
to anticipate the spiral declivity of raindrops
   the upward swoop of whirlwind,
   or the accomplishments of mist
   that folds its wings along a mountain flank;

each was an exhibition of some genius.

So it was with those that willed their fingers one yard long,
invited skin to web itself between:
this was enough, and miraculous assuredly.
Not to have planned for feathers from the outset,
   not to have begun with crossing oceans,
   not to have sacrificed
   a lesser talent than the hands—

these were the failures of invention.

So let the pterodactyl, dragonfly and bat
sweep against the eyelids of Old Earth and hang there
while new hawks and pigeons shake unwanted feathers down
for children who have hands to catch them;

the visionary cannot hold his fame forever,
nor can he avoid the execration
of his heirs and his disciples.

Thus the dark cloud settles on our hair as snow.


## THOMAS SHAPCOTT

### *Traditional Song*

When I was child and days were all
I laughed and teased and called you names
and though you used to plead and call
I would not let you share my games.
    *At last and last, December comes.*

When I was boy and days were all
I laughed and swelled to see our names
entwined in chalk upon the wall,
and longed to have you share my games.
    *At last and last, December comes.*

When I was youth and night was all
I writhed in bed and joined our names
as in your gales I dreamed to fall,
though you had never shared my games.
    *At last and last, December comes.*

When I was grown and night was all,
I learned and eased and cried Love's names:
and in my heart I heard you call
how you had let me share your games.
    *At last and last, December comes.*
    *At last and last, December comes.*

279

Now we are grown and night takes all,
I have forgotten all your names.
It is too late now to recall
we never learned each other's games.
  *At last and last, December comes.*


## *Enemies*

Stretch forth your right hand you will see
    the five betrayers move
    familiar as old love
to turn your words to perjury.


Take up your wrist and you will feel
    the armies of your blood
    rehearse the every deed
mocks at the language you can spell.


Clutch at your flesh to make the nerve
    sell out the secrets of
    such symbols as you have,
those deepest gods that you believe.


But language is the mankind thing
    that body in its heat
    is lastly caged to beat
though it rend each man's covering.

RANDOLPH STOW

## Strange Fruit

Suicide of the night—ah, flotsam:
                              (the great
poised thunderous breaker of darkness rearing above you,
and your bones awash, in the shallows, glimmering, stony,
like gods of forgotten tribes, in forgotten deserts)


take care. Take care. For your campfire falters, and firelight
folds, and will clamp around you its charcoal calyx,
and already for many hours your eyes (my terror)
have drowned in deep waters of dream, till I grow fearless.


(Embers of crocodiles love you from the mangroves.
Dingo ears yearn, yearn towards your tranquil breathing.)


Day and the firelight guard you from harm so darkly
rehearsed, removing me far; for by day I dread you,
fearing your quester's ear, that might interpret
what sings in my blood; your eye, that might guess my fever.


But so long as the harsh light lasts, I stalk your horses'
desolate spoor: a statue among the anthills,
should you look back; and prowling—and yearning, yearning,
howl out my grief and grievance, and burn in fever.


(Embers of crocodiles love you from the mangroves.
Dingo ears suck the wind for your tranquil breathing.)

I am the country's station; all else is fever.
Did we ride knee to knee down the canyons, or did I dream it?
They were lilies of dream we swam in, parrots of myth
we named for each other, 'since no-one has ever named
  them . . .'

Alone for an hour, in a thicket, I reached for strange fruit.

Now you sleep by the fire. And these are my true eyes
that glare from the swamps. And the rattling howl in the gullies
is my true voice. That cries: *You shall try strange fruit.*


## The Land's Meaning
(For Sidney Nolan)

The love of man is a weed of the waste places.
One may think of it as the spinifex of dry souls.

I have not, it is true, made the trek to the difficult country
where it is said to grow: but signs come back,
reports come back, of continuing exploration
in that terrain. And certain of our young men,
who turned in despair from the bar, upsetting a glass,
and swore: 'No more' (for the tin rooms stank of flyspray)
are sending word that the mastery of silence
alone is empire. What is God, they say,
but a man unwounded in his loneliness?

And the question (applauded, derided) falls like dust
on veranda and bar; and in pauses, when thinking ceases,
the footprints of the recently departed
march to the mind's horizons, and endure.

And often enough as we turn again, and laugh,
cloud, hide away the tracks with an acid word,
there is one or more gone past the door to stand
(wondering, debating) in the iron street,
and toss a coin, and pass, to the township's end,
where one-eyed 'Mat, eternal dealer in camels,
grins in his dusty yard like a split fruit.

But one who has returned, his eyes blurred maps
of landscapes still unmapped, gives this account:

'The third day, cockatoos dropped dead in the air.
Then the crows turned back, the camels knelt down and stayed
        there,
and a skin-coloured surf of sandhills jumped the horizon
and swamped me. I was bushed for forty years.

'And I came to a bloke all alone like a kurrajong tree.
And I said to him: "Mate—I don't need to know your name—
let me camp in your shade, let me sleep, till the sun goes
        down." '


## Landscapes

A crow cries: and the world unrolls like a blanket;
like a worn bush blanket, charred at the horizons.

But the butcherbird draws all in; that voice is a builder
of roofless cathedrals and claustrophobic forests
—and one need not notice walls, so huge is the sky.

In the morning, waking, one is most in love.
It is then that the cool convection of song and echo
wells in the clearings, and all is possible.

It is then you are not there. We meet after noon.
In the wrack of the crow. In a desert of broken quartz.

## At Sandalwood

'The love of time, and the grief of time: the harmony
of life and life in change.—In the hardest season,
praise to all three; and the crow's uniting voice
in the empty hall of the summer.'

Dead eyes have loved and changed this land I walk
in the grief of time, watching the skins of children
harden under its sun.—My sad-coloured country,
bitterly admired.

I hide, from time and the sun, on the wide veranda.
My great-grandfather's house. Out there, on the straw-brown
            sand-plain,
the christmas trees and the blackboy, tougher than ancestors,
bloom in a fume of bees.

'Love time. Love time, love lives on the grief of time.
Change defines changelessness. Hourly, on your journey,
you will turn to speak, you will find your companions altered.
Such love, such grief cannot tire.'

And the crow's voice in the empty hall of the summer
joins sun and rain, joins dust and bees; proclaiming
crows are eternal, white cockatoos are eternal:
the old names go on.


GEOFFREY LEHMANN

## The Pigs

### (For Chris Koch)

My grey-eyed father kept pigs on his farm
In Tuscany. Like troubled bowels all night
They muttered in my childhood dreams, and grumbled
Slovenly in moonlight, sprawled in night-slush,
While chill winds dried the mud upon their hides,
I lay in the faint glow of oil-lamps,
In a musk-scented stillness,
And from the icy paddocks heard the pigs.

My thoughts were haunted by pig-greed, how pigs
Surge to their food-troughs, trample on each other,
And grunt and clamber swilling themselves full.
Often we emptied food on top of them
So that they swam in muck. And then one day
When the wind splattered us with dust, my father
Heard a pig squealing, crushed beneath the press,
And we began to stone the pigs, and drew
Blood with our stones, but they just shook their buttocks,
And grunted, and still tore at cabbage leaves.

Passing a dozing boar one summer morning
My father pointed at two dead-pan eyes
Which rolled up quizzing me (and yet its head
And snout snoozed motionless, and flies
Fed and hopped undisturbed among the bristles.)
Only a pig, my father now explained,
Could glance out of the corner of its eyes.
I watch two bead-eyes turn and show
Their whites like death-flesh.


One dusk this huge old boar escaped and chased
Me through an olive-grove upon a hillside.
Dumpy, it thundered after me,
With murder in its eyes, like someone damned,
A glow of Hades perfuming the air.
That night my father took me in his arms
And told me that of all the animals
Only pigs knew of death
And knew we merely fattened them for slaughter.
Puddles of hatred against man, they wallowed
In greed, despair and viciousness,
Careless of clinging slops and vegetable scraps,
And the sows even eating their own young.
The knowledge of death made pigs into pigs.


Later that year this old boar ate
A peasant woman's baby and was burned
Alive one night by public ceremony.
My father stood there by my side,
His toga billowing in the rush of heat,
But in the flames my child-eyes saw
Not a pig, but myself,

Writhing with stump-legs and with envious eyes
Watching the men who calmly watched my death.

LES A. MURRAY

## *The Burning Truck*

(For Mrs Margaret Welton)

It began at dawn with fighter planes:
They came in off the sea and didn't rise,
They leaped the sandbar one and one and one
Coming so fast the crockery they shook down
From off my shelves was spinning in the air
When they were gone.

They came in off the sea and drew a wave
Of lagging cannon-shells across our roofs.
Windows spat glass, a truck took sudden fire,
Out leaped the driver, but the truck ran on,
Growing enormous, shambling by our street-doors,
Coming and coming . . . .

By every right in town, by every average
We knew of in the world, it had to stop,
Fetch up against a building, fall to rubble
From pure force of burning, for its whole
Body and substance were consumed with heat . . .
But stop it would not.

And all of us who knew our place and prayers
Clutched our veranda-rails and window-sills,
Begging that truck between our teeth to halt,
Keep going, vanish, strike . . . but set us free.
And then we saw the wild lads of the street
Go running after it.

And as they followed, cheering, on it crept,
Windshield melting now, canopy-frame a cage
Torn by gorillas of flame, and it kept on
Over the tramlines, past the church, on past
The last lit windows, and then out of the world
With its disciples.

# ACKNOWLEDGEMENTS

Acknowledgements and thanks are due to all the living poets, to publishers, periodicals, and other copyright holders, for permission to use the poems included in this anthology. A complete list is given below. Special thanks are due to the editors of the *Bulletin* and *Meanjin* and to Messrs Angus & Robertson for their assistance in tracing copyright holders.

Ethel Anderson:
Miss Ethel Anderson for 'Migrants'.

William Baylebridge:
The trustees of the Baylebridge estate and the Perpetual Trustee Co. of Sydney for 'The Ampler Circumscription', 'Sextains' and selections from 'Moreton Miles', 'Love Redeemed', 'A Wreath' and 'Life's Testament'.

Bruce Beaver:
Mr Bruce Beaver for 'Third Degree'.

John Blight:
Mr John Blight and Messrs Angus & Robertson for 'Sea-Level' and 'A Cup of Sea-water'.
Mr John Blight and the *Bulletin* for 'Becalmed', 'The Cat-o'-nine-tails', 'Crab' and 'Stonefish and Starfish'.

Barcroft Henry Boake:
Messrs Angus & Robertson for 'Where the Dead Men Lie'.

Christopher Brennan:
Messrs Angus & Robertson for 'We Woke Together', 'Let us Go Down', 'Sweet Silence after Bells', 'My Heart was Wandering', 'The Years that Go to Make Me Man', 'What Do I Know?', 'How Old is My Heart?', 'O Desolate Eves' and 'I Said, This Misery Must End'.

Vincent Buckley:
Professor Vincent Buckley for 'Father and Son', 'Late Tutorial', 'Secret Policeman' and 'No New Thing'.

U

David Campbell:

    Mr David Campbell for 'Night Sowing', 'Heart of Light' and 'The Monaro'.

    Mr David Campbell and Messrs Chatto and Windus for 'Men in Green' and 'Soldier's Song'.

    Mr David Campbell and Messrs Edwards & Shaw for 'Droving', 'Among the Farms' and 'Mothers and Daughters'.

Bruce Dawe:

    Mr Bruce Dawe for 'The City: Midnight', 'Freewill Offering', 'And a Good Friday was had by All' and 'To My Typewriter'.

James Devaney:

    Mr James Devaney for 'Mortality' and 'Winter Westerlies'.

Rosemary Dobson:

    Miss Rosemary Dobson for 'The Missal', 'In My End is My Beginning', 'The Devil and the Angel (1)', 'Jack' and 'The Edge'.

Max Dunn:

    Mr Max Dunn for 'Flower of Exile' and 'I Danced Before I Had Two Feet'.

Geoffrey Dutton:

    Mr Geoffrey Dutton for 'A Prisoner Freed', 'Nightflight and Sunrise' and 'January'.

William Dyson:

    Mr Daryl Lindsay as trustee of the late William Dyson's estate for 'Death is but Death'.

Mary Finnin:

    Miss Mary Finnin and the *Bulletin* for 'Sarah Lorton' and 'Three Trees at Solstice'.

Robert D. FitzGerald:

    Mr R. D. FitzGerald for 'The cock that crowed this dawn up', '1918-1941', 'The Face of the Waters', 'Traditional Tune', 'Edge', 'Song in Autumn', 'Bog and Candle' and 'This Between Us'.

Mary Fullerton:

    Messrs Angus & Robertson for 'A Dream', 'Independence', 'Passivity', 'Lovers', 'Unit' and 'Adventure'.

ACKNOWLEDGEMENTS

William Gay:
The Lothian Publishing Co. for 'The Crazy World'.

Leon Gellert:
Mr Leon Gellert for 'Before Action', 'In the Trench' and 'These Men'.

Mary Gilmore:
Dame Mary Gilmore and Messrs Angus & Robertson for 'Dedicatory', 'Of Wonder', 'Boolee, the Bringer of Life', 'The Myall in Prison', 'The Waradgery Tribe', 'The Baying Hounds', 'Nationality', 'The Dice were Loaded' and 'The Tenancy'.

Rodney Hall:
Mr Rodney Hall for 'Flight'.

Max Harris:
Mr Max Harris for 'Lullaby' and 'Martin Buber in the Pub'.

William Hart-Smith:
Mr William Hart-Smith for 'When You Touch', 'Drama', 'Baiamai's Never-failing Stream', 'Columbus Goes West' and 'Boomerang'.

Gwen Harwood:
Miss Gwen Harwood for 'O Could One Write as One Makes Love', 'Home of Mercy', 'Prize-giving' and 'Monday'.

Charles Higham:
Mr Charles Higham, *The London Magazine* and *Orient-West* (Tokyo) for 'Rushcutter's Bay'.

Edgar Holt:
Mr Edgar Holt for 'Two Sonnets from a Sequence'.

A. D. Hope:
Professor A. D. Hope for 'Australia', 'Standardization', 'Soledades of the Sun and Moon', 'A Bidding Grace', 'The Death of the Bird' and 'Crossing the Frontier'.

Peter Hopegood:
Mr Peter Hopegood for 'Free Martin' and 'Dithyramb in Retrospect'.

Rex Ingamells:
Mr Rex Ingamells for 'Sea-chronicles'.

# ACKNOWLEDGEMENTS

Eric Irvin:

Mr Eric Irvin for 'Midnight Patrol', 'Brother Ass' and 'Christmas 1942'.

Evan Jones:

Mr Evan Jones and F. W. Cheshire Pty Ltd for 'Noah's Song'.

Mr Evan Jones and Melbourne University Press for 'A Voice from Inside'.

Nancy Keesing:

Miss Nancy Keesing for 'Old Men'.

Eve Langley:

Miss Eve Langley and the *Bulletin* for 'Australia' and 'Native-born'.

Henry Lawson:

Messrs Angus & Robertson for 'The Roaring Days'.

Geoffrey Lehmann:

Mr Geoffrey Lehmann for 'The Pigs'.

J. P. McAuley:

Professor J. P. McAuley for 'Blue Horses', 'New Guinea Lament', 'Missa Papae Marcelli', 'The Death of Chiron', 'Vespers', 'To a Dead Bird of Paradise' and 'New Guinea'.

Hugh McCrae:

Messrs Angus & Robertson for 'Colombine', 'June Morning', 'Enigma', 'Song of the Rain', 'Ambuscade', 'Morning', 'The End of Desire' and 'Fragment'.

Ronald McCuaig:

Mr Ronald McCuaig for 'Betty by the Sea' and 'Love Me and Never Leave Me'.

Nan McDonald:

Miss Nan McDonald for 'Wet Summer: Botanic Gardens' and 'The Hawk'.

J. A. R. McKellar:

Messrs Angus & Robertson for 'Twelve O'Clock Boat'.

ACKNOWLEDGEMENTS

Kenneth Mackenzie:
Mr Kenneth Mackenzie and the *Bulletin* for 'Caesura' and 'Confession'.
Mr Kenneth Mackenzie and Messrs Angus & Robertson for 'Legerdemain'.
Mr Kenneth Mackenzie and F. W. Cheshire Pty Ltd for 'The Snake'.

J. S. Manifold:
Mr J. S. Manifold and Messrs Dennis Dobson Ltd for 'Fife Tune', 'Suburban Lullaby' and 'The Tomb of Lt John Learmonth, A.I.F.'.

Leonard Mann:
Mr Leonard Mann for 'The Earth' and 'Meditation in Winter'.

Ray Mathew:
Mr Ray Mathew for 'Young Man's Fancy', 'The Poems Come Easier' and 'At a Time'.

Furnley Maurice:
The Lothian Publishing Co. for selections from 'The Gully', selections from 'To God: From the Warring Nations' and 'The Victoria Markets Recollected in Tranquillity'.

E. G. Moll:
Mr E. G. Moll for 'Beware the Cuckoo' and 'On Having Grown Old'.

Ian Mudie:
Mr Ian Mudie and Georgian House for 'Underground'.
Mr Ian Mudie and Messrs Rigby Ltd for 'The North-Bound Rider'.

Les A. Murray:
Mr Les A. Murray and the Australian National University for 'The Burning Truck'.

John Shaw Neilson:
The Lothian Publishing Co. for 'Song be Delicate', 'To a Blue Flower', 'Break of Day', ' 'Tis the White Plum Tree', 'The Orange Tree', 'Stony Town', 'Schoolgirls Hastening' and 'I Spoke to the Violet'.

ACKNOWLEDGEMENTS

Bernard O'Dowd:
The Lothian Publishing Co. for 'Love and Sacrifice'.

James Picot:
Mr C. B. Christesen for 'To the Rosella in the Poinsettia Tree', 'Do You Not Hear?' and 'Finale'.

John Quinn:
Mr John Quinn for 'A Foxhole for the Night'.

Roderic Quinn:
Messrs Angus & Robertson for 'The Fisher'.

Elizabeth Riddell:
Miss Elizabeth Riddell for 'News of a Baby', 'Country Tune' and 'Forebears'.

Roland Robinson:
Mr Roland Robinson for 'Casuarina' and 'The Desert (6)'.
The *Bulletin* for 'I Breathed into the Ash' and 'The Rock-lily's Pale Spray'.

David Rowbotham:
Mr David Rowbotham for 'Mullabinda'.
Mr David Rowbotham and the *Bulletin* for 'Little White Fox'.
Mr David Rowbotham and Lyre-bird Writers for 'The Moment'.

J. R. Rowland:
Mr J. R. Rowland for 'At Noosa' and 'Seven Days'.

Thomas Shapcott:
Mr Thomas Shapcott for 'Traditional Song' and 'Enemies'.

R. A. Simpson:
Mr R. A. Simpson for 'The Death of the Devil' and 'Park Orator'.

Kenneth Slessor:
Mr Kenneth Slessor for 'Earth-Visitors', 'Stars', 'Five Visions of Captain Cook', 'Crow Country', 'Gulliver', 'Sleep', 'Five Bells' and 'Beach Burial'.

Vivian Smith:
Mr Vivian Smith for 'Bedlam Hills' and 'At an Exhibition of Historical Paintings, Hobart'.

ACKNOWLEDGEMENTS

Douglas Stewart:

Mr Douglas Stewart for 'The Silkworms'.

Mr Douglas Stewart and the *Bulletin* for 'Old Iron', 'Terra Australis', 'The Sunflowers' and 'Helmet Orchid'.

Harold Stewart:

Mr Harold Stewart for 'Dialogue of the Way'.

Randolph Stow:

Mr Randolph Stow and MacDonald & Co. Ltd for 'Strange Fruit', 'The Land's Meaning', 'Landscapes' and 'At Sandalwood'.

Colin Thiele:

Mr Colin Thiele for 'Radiation Victim' and 'TV Viewer in a Midnight Café'.

John Thompson:

Mr John Thompson for 'Letter to a Friend'.

Brian Vrepont:

Mr Brian Vrepont for 'Net-Menders' and 'The Bomber'.

Kath Walker:

Miss Kath Walker for 'Understand, Old One'.

Chris Wallace-Crabbe:

Mr Chris Wallace-Crabbe for 'Abandoned Cars' and 'Going to Sleep'.

Francis Webb:

Mr Francis Webb for 'For My Grandfather', 'The Gunner', 'Laid-Off', 'Morgan's Country', 'Cartier at St Malo', 'Five Days Old' and 'Harry'.

Judith Wright:

Miss Judith Wright for 'The Company of Lovers', 'Bullocky', 'Woman to Man', 'Woman's Song', 'Legend', 'The Ancestors' and 'The Harp and the King'.

# SOURCES OF THE POEMS

Charles Harpur:
  'A Midsummer Noon in the Australian Forest' from *Poems*, George
    Robertson, 1883.

Daniel Deniehy:
  'To His Wife' from *An Australasian Anthology*, Collins, 1946.

Henry Kendall:
  'Prefatory Sonnet' from *Leaves from Australian Forests*, George
    Robertson, 1869.

William Gay:
  'The Crazy World' from *The Poetical Works of William Gay*, Lothian,
    1911.

Barcroft Henry Boake:
  'Where the Dead Men Lie' from *Where the Dead Men Lie*, Angus &
    Robertson, 1913.

Bernard O'Dowd:
  'Love and Sacrifice' from *Collected Poems of Bernard O'Dowd*,
    Lothian, 1941.

Henry Lawson:
  'The Roaring Days' from *The Poetical Works of Henry Lawson*, Angus
    & Robertson, 1944.

Christopher Brennan:
  'We Woke Together' from *XXI Poems*, Angus & Robertson, 1897.
  'Let us Go Down' from *Poems*, G. B. Philp & Son, 1913.
  'Sweet Silence after Bells' from *Poems*, G. B. Philp & Son, 1913.
  'My Heart was Wandering' from *Poems*, G. B. Philp & Son, 1913.
  'The Years that Go to Make Me Man' from *Poems*, G. B. Philp
    & Son, 1913.
  'What Do I Know?' from *Poems*, G. B. Philp & Son, 1913.
  'How Old is My Heart?' from *Poems*, G. B. Philp & Son, 1913.
  'O Desolate Eves' from *Poems*, G. B. Philp & Son, 1913.
  'I Said, This Misery Must End' from *Poems*, G. B. Philp & Son,
    1913.

John Shaw Neilson:

'Song be Delicate' from *Collected Poems*, Lothian, 1934.

'To a Blue Flower' from *Collected Poems*, Lothian, 1934.

'Break of Day' from *Collected Poems*, Lothian, 1934.

''Tis the White Plum Tree' from *Collected Poems*, Lothian, 1934.

'The Orange Tree' from *Collected Poems*, Lothian, 1934.

'Stony Town' from *Collected Poems*, Lothian, 1934.

'Schoolgirls Hastening' from *Collected Poems*, Lothian, 1934.

'I Spoke to the Violet' from *Beauty Imposes*, Angus & Robertson, 1938.

William Dyson:

'Death is but Death' from *Poems in Memory of a Wife*, Cecil Palmer, 1919.

Leon Gellert:

'Before Action' from *Songs of a Campaign*, G. Hassell & Co., 1917.

'In the Trench' from *Songs of a Campaign*, G. Hassell & Co., 1917.

'These Men' from *Songs of a Campaign*, G. Hassell & Co., 1917.

Furnley Maurice:

'To God: From the Warring Nations' (selections) from *Poems*, Lothian, 1944.

'The Gully' (selections) from *Poems*, Lothian, 1944.

'The Victoria Markets Recollected in Tranquillity' from *Poems*, Lothian, 1944.

William Baylebridge:

'Wherever I Go' from *Selected Poems*, Gordon & Gotch, 1919.

'The utile canons, the set codes of priests' from *Love Redeemed*, Tallabila Press, 1939.

'Who questions if the punctual sun unbars' from *Love Redeemed*, Tallabila Press, 1939.

'When tongues will tax me in the public ear' from *A Wreath*, privately printed, c.1939.

'The Ampler Circumscription' from *This Vital Flesh*, Tallabila Press, 1939.

'The brain, the blood, the busy thews' from *This Vital Flesh*, Tallabila Press, 1939.

'I worshipped, when my veins were fresh' from *This Vital Flesh*, Tallabila Press, 1939.

'All that I am to Earth belongs' from *This Vital Flesh*, Tallabila Press, 1939.

'Into ethereal meads' from *This Vital Flesh*, Tallabila Press, 1939.

'Sextains' (two poems) from *Sextains*, Tallabila Press, 1939.

Mary Gilmore:

'Dedicatory' from *Selected Verse*, Angus & Robertson, 1948.
'Of Wonder' from *Selected Verse*, Angus & Robertson, 1948.
'Boolee, the Bringer of Life' from *Selected Verse*, Angus & Robertson, 1948.
'The Myall in Prison' from *Selected Verse*, Angus & Robertson, 1948.
'The Waradgery Tribe' from *Selected Verse*, Angus & Robertson, 1948.
'The Baying Hounds' from *Selected Verse*, Angus & Robertson, 1948.
'Nationality' from *Fourteen Men*, Angus & Robertson, 1954.
'The Dice were Loaded' from *Selected Verse*, Angus & Robertson, 1948.
'The Tenancy' from *Selected Verse*, Angus & Robertson, 1948.

Mary Fullerton:

'A Dream' from *Moles Do So Little with Their Privacy*, Angus & Robertson, 1942.
'Independence' from *Moles Do So Little with Their Privacy*, Angus & Robertson, 1942.
'Passivity' from *Moles Do So Little with Their Privacy*, Angus & Robertson, 1942.
'Lovers' from *Moles Do So Little with Their Privacy*, Angus & Robertson, 1942.
'Unit' from *Moles Do So Little with Their Privacy*, Angus & Robertson, 1942.
'Adventure' from *Moles Do So Little with Their Privacy*, Angus & Robertson, 1942.

Roderic Quinn:

'The Fisher' from *Poems*, Angus & Robertson, 1920.

James Devaney:

'Mortality' from *Poems*, Angus & Robertson, 1950.
'Winter Westerlies' from *Poems*, Angus & Robertson, 1950.

Hugh McCrae:

'Colombine' from *Colombine*, Angus & Robertson, 1920.
'June Morning' from *Colombine*, Angus & Robertson, 1920.
'Enigma' from *Colombine*, Angus & Robertson, 1920.
'Song of the Rain' from *Colombine*, Angus & Robertson, 1920.
'Ambuscade' from *Satyrs and Sunlight*, Fanfrolico Press, 1928.
'Morning' from *Satyrs and Sunlight*, Fanfrolico Press, 1928.
'The End of Desire' from *Satyrs and Sunlight*, Fanfrolico Press, 1928.
'Fragment' from *Australian Poetry*, Angus & Robertson, 1944.

Leonard Mann:
'The Earth' from *Poems from the Mask*, Hawthorn Press, 1951.
'Meditation in Winter' from *The Delectable Mountains*, Angus & Robertson, 1944.

E. G. Moll:
'Beware the Cuckoo' from *Beware the Cuckoo*, Australasian Publishing Co., 1947.
'On Having Grown Old' from *The Lifted Spear*, Angus & Robertson, 1953.

Kenneth Slessor:
'Earth-Visitors' from *One Hundred Poems*, Angus & Robertson, 1944.
'Stars' from *One Hundred Poems*, Angus & Robertson, 1944.
'Five Visions of Captain Cook' from *One Hundred Poems*, Angus & Robertson, 1944.
'Crow Country' from *One Hundred Poems*, Angus & Robertson, 1944.
'Gulliver' from *One Hundred Poems*, Angus & Robertson, 1944.
'Sleep' from *One Hundred Poems*, Angus & Robertson, 1944.
'Five Bells' from *One Hundred Poems*, Angus & Robertson, 1944.
'Beach Burial' from *Australian Poetry*, Angus & Robertson, 1944.

John Thompson:
'Letter to a Friend' from *Thirty Poems*, Edwards & Shaw, 1954.

R. D. FitzGerald:
'The cock that crowed this dawn up' from *Moonlight Acre*, Melbourne University Press, 1938.
'1918-1941' from *This Night's Orbit*, Melbourne University Press, 1953.
'The Face of the Waters' from *This Night's Orbit*, Melbourne University Press, 1953.
'Traditional Tune' from *This Night's Orbit*, Melbourne University Press, 1953.
'Edge' from *Southmost Twelve*, Angus & Robertson, 1962.
'Song in Autumn' from *Southmost Twelve*, Angus & Robertson, 1962.
'Bog and Candle' from *Southmost Twelve*, Angus & Robertson, 1962.
'This Between Us . . .' from *Southmost Twelve*, Angus & Robertson, 1962.

J. A. R. McKellar:
'Twelve O'Clock Boat' from *Collected Poems*, Angus & Robertson, 1946.

Ethel Anderson:
'Migrants' from *Australian Poetry*, Angus & Robertson, 1949.

Peter Hopegood:
'Free Martin' from *Thirteen from Oahu*, Frank Johnson, 1940.
'Dithyramb in Retrospect' from *Circus at World's End*, Angus & Robertson, 1947.

Max Dunn:
'Flower of Exile' from *Time of Arrival*, privately printed.
'I Danced Before I Had Two Feet' from *Australia Writes*, Cheshire, 1953.

Brian Vrepont:
'Net-menders' from *Beyond the Claw*, Angus & Robertson, 1952.
'The Bomber' from *Australian Poetry*, Angus & Robertson, 1946.

A. D. Hope:
'Australia' from *Poems*, Hamish Hamilton, 1960.
'Standardization' from *The Wandering Islands*, Edwards & Shaw, 1955.
'Soledades of the Sun and Moon' from *Poems*, Hamish Hamilton, 1960.
'A Bidding Grace' from *Poems*, Hamish Hamilton, 1960.
'The Death of the Bird' from *Poems*, Hamish Hamilton, 1960.
'Crossing the Frontier' from *Collected Poems 1930-1965*, Angus & Robertson, 1966.

Ronald McCuaig:
'Betty by the Sea' from *Quod Ronald McCuaig*, Angus & Robertson, 1946.
'Love Me and Never Leave Me' from *Quod Ronald McCuaig*, Angus & Robertson, 1946.

James Picot:
'To the Rosella in the Poinsettia Tree' from *With a Hawk's Quill*, Meanjin Press, 1954.
'Do You Not Hear?' from *With a Hawk's Quill*, Meanjin Press, 1954.
'Finale' from *With a Hawk's Quill*, Meanjin Press, 1954.

Ian Mudie:
'Underground' from *Poems 1934-1944*, Georgian House, 1945.
'The North-Bound Rider' from *The North-Bound Rider*, Rigby, 1963.

Rex Ingamells:
'Sea-chronicles' from *Australian Poetry*, Angus & Robertson, 1947.

William Hart-Smith:
'When You Touch' from *Harvest*, Jindyworobak Press, 1943.
'Drama' from *Jindyworobak Anthology*, 1943.
'Baiamai's Never-failing Stream' from *Harvest*, Jindyworobak Press, 1943.
'Columbus Goes West' from *Christopher Columbus*, Caxton Press, 1948.
'Boomerang' from *Poems of Discovery*, Angus & Robertson, 1959.

Roland Robinson:
'Casuarina' from *Language of the Sand*, Lyre-bird Writers, 1949.
'I Breathed into the Ash' from *Tumult of the Swans*, Lyre-bird Writers, 1953.
'The Rock-lily's Pale Spray' from *Tumult of the Swans*, Lyre-bird Writers, 1953.
'The Desert (6)' from *Deep Well*, Edwards & Shaw, 1962.

Elizabeth Riddell:
'News of a Baby' from *Poems*, Ure Smith, 1948.
'Country Tune' from *Forebears*, Angus & Robertson, 1961.
'Forebears' from *Forebears*, Angus & Robertson, 1961.

John Quinn:
'A Foxhole for the Night' from *Australian Poetry*, Angus & Robertson, 1945.

Douglas Stewart:
'Old Iron' from *The Dosser in Springtime*, Angus & Robertson, 1946.
'Terra Australis' from *Sun Orchids*, Angus & Robertson, 1952.
'The Sunflowers' from *Sun Orchids*, Angus & Robertson, 1952.
'Helmet Orchid' from *Sun Orchids*, Angus & Robertson, 1952.
'The Silkworms' from *Rutherford*, Angus & Robertson, 1962.

Eve Langley:
'Native-born' from the *Bulletin*.
'Australia' from the *Bulletin*.

Kenneth Mackenzie:
'Confession' from *The Moonlit Doorway*, Angus & Robertson, 1944.
'Caesura' from *Selected Poems*, Angus & Robertson, 1961.
'The Snake' from *Selected Poems*, Angus & Robertson, 1961.
'Legerdemain' from *Selected Poems*, Angus & Robertson, 1961.

John Blight:

'Becalmed' from *The Two Suns Met*, Lyre-bird Writers, 1954.
'The Cat-o'-nine-tails' from *The Two Suns Met*, Lyre-bird Writers, 1954.
'Crab' from *A Beachcomber's Diary*, Angus & Robertson, 1963.
'Stonefish and Starfish' from *A Beachcomber's Diary*, Angus & Robertson, 1963.
'Sea-Level' from *A Beachcomber's Diary*, Angus & Robertson, 1963.
'A Cup of Sea-water' from *A Beachcomber's Diary*, Angus & Robertson, 1963.

Harold Stewart:

'Dialogue of the Way' from *Meanjin*.

J. P. McAuley:

'The Blue Horses' from *Under Aldebaran*, Melbourne University Press, 1947.
'New Guinea Lament' from *Under Aldebaran*, Melbourne University Press, 1947.
'Missa Papae Marcelli' from *Under Aldebaran*, Melbourne University Press, 1947.
'The Death of Chiron' from *A Vision of Ceremony*, Angus & Robertson, 1956.
'Vespers' from *A Vision of Ceremony*, Angus & Robertson, 1956.
'To a Dead Bird of Paradise' from *A Vision of Ceremony*, Angus & Robertson, 1956.
'New Guinea' from *A Vision of Ceremony*, Angus & Robertson, 1956.

Eric Irvin:

'Midnight Patrol' from *Australian Poetry*, Angus & Robertson, 1944.
'Brother Ass' from *Australian Poetry*, Angus & Robertson, 1947.
'Christmas 1942' from *A Soldier's Miscellany*, Angus & Robertson, 1945.

Edgar Holt:

'Two Sonnets from a Sequence' from *Meanjin*.

J. S. Manifold:

'Fife Tune' from *Selected Verse*, Dennis Dobson, 1948.
'Suburban Lullaby' from *Selected Verse*, Dennis Dobson, 1948.
'The Tomb of Lt John Learmonth, A.I.F.' from *Selected Verse* Dennis Dobson, 1948.

Judith Wright:

'The Company of Lovers' from *The Moving Image*, Meanjin Press, 1946.

'Bullocky' from *The Moving Image*, Meanjin Press, 1946.

'Woman to Man' from *Woman to Man*, Angus & Robertson, 1949.

'Woman's Song' from *Woman to Man*, Angus & Robertson, 1949.

'Legend' from *The Gateway*, Angus & Robertson, 1953.

'The Ancestors' from *The Gateway*, Angus & Robertson, 1953.

'The Harp and the King' from *The Two Fires*, Angus & Robertson, 1955.

David Campbell:

'Soldier's Song' from *Speak with the Sun*, Chatto & Windus, 1949.

'Men in Green' from *Speak with the Sun*, Chatto & Windus, 1949.

'Night Sowing' from *The Miracle of Mullion Hill*, Angus & Robertson, 1956.

'Heart of Light' from *The Miracle of Mullion Hill*, Angus & Robertson, 1956.

'The Monaro' from *The Miracle of Mullion Hill*, Angus & Robertson, 1956.

'Droving' from *Poems*, Edwards & Shaw, 1962.

'Among the Farms' from *Poems*, Edwards & Shaw, 1962.

'Mothers and Daughters' from *Poems*, Edwards & Shaw, 1962.

Rosemary Dobson:

'The Missal' from *In a Convex Mirror*, Dymocks, 1944.

'In my End is my Beginning' from *The Ship of Ice*, Angus & Robertson, 1948.

'The Devil and the Angel (1)' from *The Ship of Ice*, Angus & Robertson, 1948.

'Jack' from *Cockcrow*, Angus & Robertson, 1965.

'The Edge' from *Cockcrow*, Angus & Robertson, 1965.

Nan McDonald:

'Wet Summer: Botanic Gardens' from *The Lonely Fire*, Angus & Robertson, 1954.

'The Hawk' from *The Lighthouse*, Angus & Robertson, 1959.

Nancy Keesing:

'Old Men' from *Imminent Summer*, Lyre-bird Writers, 1951.

David Rowbotham:

'Little White Fox' from *Inland*, Angus & Robertson, 1958.

'The Moment' from *Ploughman and Poet*, Lyre-bird Writers, 1954.

'Mullabinda' from *Inland*, Angus & Robertson, 1958.

Mary Finnin:
  'Sarah Lorton' from the *Bulletin*.
  'Three Trees at Solstice' from the *Bulletin*.

Max Harris:
  'Lullaby' from *The Coorong*, Mary Martin Bookshop, 1955.
  'Martin Buber in the Pub' from *The Coorong*, Mary Martin Book-
    shop, 1955.

Geoffrey Dutton:
  'Nightflight and Sunrise' from *Nightflight and Sunrise*, Reed &
    Harris, 1944.
  'A Prisoner Freed' from *Australian Poetry*, Angus & Robertson,
    1944.
  'January' from *Flowers and Fury*, Cheshire, 1962.

Francis Webb:
  'For My Grandfather' from *Leichhardt in Theatre*, Angus & Robert-
    son, 1952.
  'The Gunner' from *Leichhardt in Theatre*, Angus & Robertson, 1952.
  'Laid-Off' from *Birthday*, privately printed.
  'Morgan's Country' from *Leichhardt in Theatre*, Angus & Robertson,
    1952.
  'Cartier at St Malo' from *Leichhardt in Theatre*, Angus & Robertson,
    1952.
  'Five Days Old' from *Socrates*, Angus & Robertson, 1961.
  'Harry' from *The Ghost of the Cock*, Angus & Robertson, 1964.

Vincent Buckley:
  'Father and Son' from *Masters in Israel*, Angus & Robertson, 1961.
  'Late Tutorial' from *Masters in Israel*, Angus & Robertson, 1961.
  'Secret Policeman' from *Eight by Eight*, Jacaranda Press, 1963.
  'No New Thing' from *Eight by Eight*, Jacaranda Press, 1963.

Ray Mathew:
  'Young Man's Fancy' from *Song and Dance*, Lyre-bird Writers, 1956.
  'The Poems come Easier' from *With Cypress Pine*, Lyre-bird Writers,
    1951.
  'At a Time' from *South of the Equator*, Angus & Robertson, 1961.

Gwen Harwood:
  'O Could One Write as One Makes Love' from *Poems*, Angus &
    Robertson, 1963.
  'Home of Mercy' from *Poems*, Angus & Robertson, 1963.
  'Prize-giving' from *Poems*, Angus & Robertson, 1963.

V

Francis Geyer:
'Monday' from the *Bulletin*.

Kath Walker:
'Understand, Old One' from *The Dawn Is at Hand*, Jacaranda Press, 1966.

Colin Thiele:
'Radiation Victim' from *In Charcoal and Conté*, Rigby, 1966.
'TV Viewer in a Midnight Café' from *In Charcoal and Conté*, Rigby, 1966.

J. R. Rowland:
'At Noosa' from *A Feast of Ancestors*, Angus & Robertson, 1965.
'Seven Days' from *A Feast of Ancestors*, Angus & Robertson, 1965.

Bruce Beaver:
'Third Degree' from *Seawall and Shoreline*, South Head Press, 1964.

R. A. Simpson:
'The Death of the Devil' from *This Real Pompeii*, Jacaranda Press, 1964.
'Park Orator' from *This Real Pompeii*, Jacaranda Press, 1964.

Bruce Dawe:
'The City: Midnight' from *No Fixed Address*, Cheshire, 1962.
'Freewill Offering' from *A Need of Similar Name*, Cheshire, 1965.
'And a Good Friday was had by All' from *A Need of Similar Name*, Cheshire, 1965.
'To My Typewriter' from *A Need of Similar Name*, Cheshire, 1965.

Charles Higham:
'Rushcutter's Bay' from *Noonday Country*, Angus & Robertson, 1966.

Evan Jones:
'Noah's Song' from *Inside the Whale*, Cheshire, 1960.
'A Voice from Inside' from *Understandings*, Melbourne University Press, 1967.

Vivian Smith:
'Bedlam Hills' from *The Other Meaning*, Edwards & Shaw, 1956.
'At an Exhibition of Historical Paintings, Hobart' from *Australian Poetry*, Angus & Robertson, 1965.

306

SOURCES OF THE POEMS

Chris Wallace-Crabbe:

'Abandoned Cars' from *In Light and Darkness*, Angus & Robertson, 1963.

'Going to Sleep' from *In Light and Darkness*, Angus & Robertson, 1963.

Rodney Hall:

'Flight' from *The Autobiography of a Gorgon* (not yet published).

Thomas Shapcott:

'Traditional Song' from *Time on Fire*, Jacaranda Press, 1961.

'Enemies' from *The Mankind Thing*, Jacaranda Press, 1964.

Randolph Stow:

'Strange Fruit' from *The Outrider*, MacDonald, 1962.

'The Land's Meaning' from *The Outrider*, MacDonald, 1962.

'Landscapes' from *The Outrider*, MacDonald, 1962.

'At Sandalwood' from *The Outrider*, MacDonald, 1962.

Geoffrey Lehmann:

'The Pigs' from *The Ilex Tree*, Australian National University, 1965.

Les A. Murray:

'The Burning Truck' from *The Ilex Tree*, Australian National University, 1965.

# INDEX OF AUTHORS AND TITLES

(Note: For the purpose of this index authors are included under their own names, where they have used a pseudonym for writing purposes.)

# INDEX OF FIRST LINES

# Hush, little baby ...

The air in the old house was stuffy. Charli let the door click shut behind her, shutting out the sound of kids playing across the street. Silence settled around her like a blanket. . . . The room had a funny smell, like dead flowers. Dead something.

She was about to turn back when a movement caught her eye. The expanse of wall opposite the windows was no longer bare. Against the dingy wallpaper lay the shadow of a cradle, as sharply outlined as if it were painted there. Her astonishment deepened to panic as the shadow grew larger and darker. And there was something else. . . .

There was the shadow of a cradle, but no cradle. The shadow had kept growing and darkening. And then it had rocked, as if an invisible hand were moving it.

**Iowa Children's Choice Award Master List**

**Society of School Librarians
International Honor Book**